Rabbi Akiva,
Bar Kokhba Revolt,
and the
Ten Tribes of Israel

Rabbi Akiva, Bar Kokhba Revolt, and the Ten Tribes of Israel

Alexander Zephyr

iUniverse LLC
Bloomington

RABBI AKIVA, BAR KOKHBA REVOLT, AND THE TEN TRIBES OF ISRAEL

iUniverse books may be ordered through booksellers or by contacting:

iUniverse LLC
1663 Liberty Drive
Bloomington, IN 47403
www.iuniverse.com
1-800-Authors (1-800-288-4677)

ISBN: 978-1-4917-1256-6 (sc)
ISBN: 978-1-4917-1257-3 (e)

Library of Congress Control Number: 2013920320

Printed in the United States of America.

iUniverse rev. date: 01/06/2014

CONTENTS

INTRODUCTION

The 'Lost' Ten Tribes of Israel
are Destined to Return

Will the lost Ten Tribes of Israel ever reunite with the remaining Jews and return to the God of their fathers and to the Promised Land? R. Akiva, 'The Chief of all Sages,' answers in the negative: "The ten tribes will not return. Just as a day passes and it will never return so too, they will be exiled never to return." His teacher and opponent, R. Eliezer, responds to the same question in the affirmative: "Just like a day is followed by darkness, and the light later returns, so too, although it will become dark for the ten tribes, God will ultimately take them out of their darkness" (Talmud, Sanhedrin 110b).

Of course, there are some scholars who have attempted to reconcile the commonly unaccepted negative position of Rabbi Akiva towards the Ten Tribes by saying that what he meant is that most of the Ten Tribes had already returned during the time of the Second Temple: the remainder of the Ten Tribes is lost forever and will never return (Rabbi Joseph Albo, 1380-1444 CE, *Sefer ha-Ikkarim* 4:42). The other commentators say that R. Akiva was misunderstood. What he actually said is that the original generation of the exiled Ten Tribes (or Generation of the Wilderness, as it is sometimes called) would not be resurrected and stands in Judgment, but rather that their future descendants would.

But even this narrow interpretation of R. Akiva's position was strongly refuted by R. Eliezer the Great: "They [the Generation of the Wilderness] will enter into the future world, for it is written, 'Gather My saints together unto Me; those that have made a covenant with Me by sacrifice'" (Sanhedrin 110b; Exodus 24:5, 8). Rabbah b. Bar Hana expressed the same critical opinion of R. Akiva's position concerning the cursed 'Generation of the Wilderness,' saying in R. Johanan's name: "[Here] R. Akiba abandoned his love. For it is written, 'Go and cry in the ears of Jerusalem, saying, Thus saith the Lord: I remember thee, the kindness of thy youth, the love of thine espousals, when thou wentest *after Me in the wilderness*, in a land that was not sown; if others will enter [the future world] in their merit, *surely they themselves most certainly will!*'" (Babylonian Talmud: Tractate Sanhedrin, 110b; Jeremiah 2:2, emphasis mine).

These interpretations are not really reflective what R. Akiva meant. Why would the other great sages, such as R. Eliezer, R. Yehudah the Prince, and the rabbis of the Talmud, have understood him correctly and uncompromisingly argued against his statement? R. Akiva himself forestalled any such speculations by introducing a very powerful example of a widow whose husband died naturally or was killed and never came back to her (Eichah Rabbah 1:3). This parable strengthened his position that the Ten Tribes will never come back and will not have a part in the World-To-Come (Rabbi Don Yitzchak Abarbanel, 1437-1508 CE, Yeshuot Meshicho, Iyun 1:4).

Rabbah Bar Hana said in R. Johanan's name: "[Here] R. Akiva abandoned his love, for it is written, 'Go and proclaim these words toward the north, and say, Return, thou backsliding Israel, saith the Lord; and I will not cause mine anger to fall upon you; for I am merciful, saith the Lord, and I will not keep mine anger forever'" (Jeremiah 3:12). The rabbi's answer shows that he, and others of his day, perfectly understood R. Akiva's position towards the Ten Tribes to apply not only to the sinful 'Generation of the Wilderness' but rather to the 'lost' backsliding Israel in exile from the north.

The negative position of Rabbi Akiva contradicts the teachings of the Bible (Tanakh), the Talmud, and the sages, of whose opinions he undoubtedly had been aware. Despite that, this great scholar continued with incredible incomprehensibility to defend his negative conclusion towards the Ten Tribes: "All Israel will be admitted to the future world, with the exception of the generation of the Wilderness and the Ten Lost Tribes" (Tractate Sanhedrin xi. 3; 110b).

Too Many 'Whys'

Why did Rabbi Akiva take such a consistently unjust attitude towards the Ten Tribes? The Talmud itself seems to disagree with his position and reprimands Rabbi Akiva for his view, saying that *"shavkah Rabbi Akiva lechasiduteh."* In other words, Rabbi Akiva had abandoned his usual spirit of kindness and generosity; he would usually try to exonerate the Jewish people. (Note: *the Ten Tribes of Israel are not the Jewish people but rather their brother Israelites, who separated from them, were exiled, and lost their national identity*).

To properly understand R. Akiva's negative position concerning the return of the Ten Tribes, we need to understand the life and deeds of this great man. It may also be helpful to ask some unexpected questions: Why were his closest disciples, R. Simeon ben Yochai and R. Meir, against his position regarding the Ten Tribes? R. Simeon b. Judah, of the Kefar of Acco, said on R. Simeon's authority: "If their deeds are as this day's, they will not return; otherwise they shall" (Sanhedrin 110b). His words indicate that R. Simeon ben Judah, R. Simeon ben Yochai, and R. Meir made the return of the Ten Tribes conditional upon their repentance. If they repented, God would bring them back. The Bible verses teach precisely the same message.

Why did R. Eliezer the Great, the mentor and teacher of Rabbi Akiva, consistently oppose him on many occasions? Rabbi Eliezer contradicted him on different matters of Torah, and especially on this very subject of Israel's return. R. Eliezer said: "I never taught anything which I had not learned from my masters" (Sukkah 28a). Who was his teacher? It was none other than the much-revered wise man of Israel, Rabbi Yohanan ben Zakkai! The Talmud instructs those searching justice and truth: "Seek a reliable court; go after R. Eliezer to Lydda or after Johanan ben Zakkai to Beror Hel" (Sanhedrin 32b). The brilliant editor of the Mishnah, R. Yehudah Ha Nasi (The Prince, 135-219 CE), known as Rebbi or *Rabbeinu HaKadosh* (which in Hebrew means 'our Master, the holy one') also rejected R. Akiva's opinion, saying *"The ten tribes are destined for the World to come"* [emphasis mine]. R. Akiva's explanations of the idea that Ten Tribes will not return are ultimately theologically shallow (cf. Deuteronomy 29:28; Leviticus 26:38), reminding one of the practice, so common among Christian fundamentalists, of taking verses out of context in order to prove a point.

What the Biblical Verses Say

Let us take a look at the passage from Deuteronomy 29:28: "And the LORD rooted them out of their land *in anger*, and *in wrath*, and *in great indignation*, and cast them into another land, as *it is* this day" [italics added]. R. Akiva claimed that the pronoun 'they' refers to the Ten Tribes. He has been understood to mean: 'As *it is* this day' is to be read to signify forever, implying that the Ten

Tribes will be exiled in perpetuity. As mentioned earlier, R. Akiva even gave an example of a widow whose husband died naturally or was killed and never come back to her, so as to strengthen his position that the Ten Tribes would never come back and will not have a part in the World-To-Come (Eichah Rabbah 1:3).

What was God's reason for delivering such a harsh punishment? Here is the answer: "For they went and served other gods, and worshipped them, gods whom they knew not, and whom He had not given to them. And the anger of the LORD was kindled against this land, to bring on it all the curses that are written in this book" (Deuteronomy 29:26-27).

R. Akiva's attitude is all the more distressing when we see that the very next chapter of Deuteronomy fully retracts God's conditional curses against Israel and speaks of God's blessings awaiting Israel if its people repent and turn to God: "Then the LORD your God will return you from captivity, and have compassion upon you, and will return and gather you from all the nations, where the LORD your God has scattered you" (30:3). This passage explains why R. Simeon ben Judah, R. Simeon ben Yochai, and R. Meir taught that the return of the Ten Tribes depends on their repentance.

This is exactly what God says: "But from there you shall seek HaShem your God, and shall find, when you search for Him with all your heart and with all your being. For HaShem your God is a compassionate God, He does not forsake you, nor destroy you, nor forget the covenant of your fathers which He swore to them" (Deuteronomy 4:29-31).

As Joseph revealed his identity with loud cry to shocking brothers in the land of Egypt (Genesis 45:1-2), so it would be in the future when the descendants of Joseph, who represent the Ten Tribes, with cry and joy come to Judah for reunification, "With cries they will come, and with mercy I will lead them" (Jeremiah 31:8). As in the past, the Jewish nation will be in a shock to see this magnificent Exodus of multitude Israelites of the Ten Tribes coming to join them. Their hearts will be thrilled and exulted with joy and their eyes will shine. "Then shalt thou say in thine heart, who hath begotten me these, seeing I have lost my children, and am desolate, a captive, and removing to and fro? And who hath brought up these? Behold, I was left alone; these, where had they been" (Isaiah 49:21)? What a precise description of this touching moment!

For R. Akiva to say that the Ten Tribes will not return is equivalent to stating that Ten Tribes will never repent and acknowledge the God of their fathers and His live-giving Torah; that they will never reunite with the rest of their brothers and sisters of the whole House of Israel in the days of Moshiach and never be redeemed by the Almighty. It also implies denial of God's prophets, the Hebrew Bible, the Great Sages, the Talmud, Rabbinical literature, and more, all of which speak positively of the Messiah and the return of the Ten Tribes. How can they all be wrong? Is everyone mistaken except for Rabbi Akiva?

The truth is that Judaism does not esteem the Talmud as being holier than the Bible. There is a great difference between the Bible, which is the Sacred Word of God, and the Talmud compiled by men (no matter how wise they are), discussing traditions and the logic of interpretation. The Talmud explains the Bible: It is not suppose to contradict it.

Let us compare the verse of Deuteronomy 29:28 with a verse from Jeremiah, "Behold, *I will gather them out of all countries,* whither I have driven them in mine *anger,* and in My *fury,* and in *great wrath*; and I will bring them again unto this place, and I will cause them to dwell safely" (32:37, emphasis mine). Is this not a direct answer to R. Akiva's negative position? The Ten Tribes will definitely return if we use the Tanakh as our guide. Or consider this passage: "For thus says the Lord GOD; Behold, I, even I, will both search for my sheep, and seek them out. And I will bring them out from the people, and gather them from the countries, and will bring them to their own land, and feed them upon the mountains of Israel by the rivers, and in all the inhabited places of the country" (Ezekiel 34:11,13). In the Tanakh there are numerous passages where God makes it perfectly clear that there will be a reunification and redemption of the two Houses of Judah and Israel in the time of the Messiah. Those who reject these prophecies reject the sacred Word of the Almighty.

The same goes for further so-called evidence that R. Akiva uses to justify his position. Let us turn to Leviticus, a verse of which reads, "And you shall perish among the nations, and the land of your enemies shall eat you up" (26:38). Before considering the verse, let us first place it in the context of the chapter as a whole. In short, it consists of the blessings with which God will reward the Israelites for obedience and keeping His Laws, as well as the curses for rejecting God and His Torah. After naming the curses, God says that Israel will repent and return to Him. God will punish its people, but never break His Covenant. R. Akiva cites, as proof of his negative position towards return of the Ten Tribes, the following passage from Leviticus: "And you shall perish among the nations, and the land of your enemies shall eat you up" (26:38).

This curse against the Israelites for disobedience is, as mentioned, followed by the verses of blessings consequent to repentance:

"But they will confess their sins and the sins of their fathers. And yet for all that, when they be in the land of their enemies, *I will not cast them away,* neither will I abhor them, to destroy them utterly, and to break My covenant with them: for I am the LORD their God. But I will for their sakes remember the covenant of their ancestors, whom I brought forth out of the land of Egypt in the sight of the heathen, that I might be their God: I am the LORD" (emphasis mine, Leviticus 26:40, 44).

To ignore these Words of Almighty and say that the Ten Tribes will never return to the God of their fathers, to His immortal Torah, to the Promised Land, and that they will not have a part in a future world, would seem to verge on blasphemy. R. Akiva's defense of his position that the Ten Tribes will not return and will not merit the Judgment Day and life in the World-to-come (Leviticus 26:28; Deuteronomy 28:29) does not, then, hold ground. It is refuted by Scriptural and Rabbinical sources. Similarly he explains the Egyptian curse of the frogs ('But if you refuse to let them go, behold, I will smite all your territory with frogs') in Exodus 8:2 as meaning that only one frog came forth and then subdivided multiple times. Of this interpretation, Rabbi Eleazar ben Azariah was openly critical: "Akiva, why do you not stick to the laws of purity, and leave *Aggadah* alone?" (Babylonian Talmud, Chagiga 14a), by which he simply meant that R. Akiva was not considered an authority in the realm of *Aggadah* (e.g. legends, homiletic explanations) and was advised to occupy himself instead with *halakhah* (e.g. the practical application of Law).

If the Ten Tribes have disappeared, it will be impossible to fulfill future prophecies of Reunification, Redemption, and the Messianic Age, which in turn suggests that the Bible is not the holy Word of God. If they have not disappeared, they will have lost their identity. Obviously, they must be around, waiting for the time when Divine Providence will bring them back to the Almighty God of Israel and to His Divine Laws.

Concerning the Ten Tribes and their future return, it is not a secret that the 'lost' Ten Tribes will have become a different entity than Judah. Scripture says they will be speaking a foreign language (Isaiah 28:11) and will bear another name (Isaiah 65:15). Throughout the ages Israel has been punished by God for its transgressions. But this situation will not continue forever, "For thus said the LORD; like as I have brought all this great evil upon this people, so will I bring upon them all the good that I have promised them" (Jeremiah 32:42). The Almighty will not let His people completely degenerate into idolatry and become a 'Wilderness of the nations' like the surrounding Heathen nations: "And that which comes into your mind shall not be at all, that you say, We will be as the Gentiles, as the families of the countries, to serve wood and stone" (Ezekiel 20:32).

The Destiny of Israel

The destiny of Israel is better than this. They will become a holy nation of priests, a light to the Gentiles. They will bring salvation and the glory of the God of Israel to the ends of the Earth (Isaiah 49:6). All of these things will pass in the time of the Messianic Age. Israel will never be forgotten or rejected by God, whose Covenant cannot be broken. (Judges 2:1; Leviticus 26:44; Psalms 111:5; Jer. 31:36). "Hear the word of the LORD, O you nations, and declare it in the coastlands afar off, and say, He that scattered Israel will gather him, and keep him, as a shepherd does his flock (Jeremiah 31:10). The Mishnah (Tractate Sanhedrin 11:1) says: "All Israelites have a share in the World-to-Come, as it is says, 'Your people also shall be all righteous, they shall inherit the Land for ever; the branch of My planting, the work of My hands, that I may be glorified'" (Isaiah 60:21). It does not say here that only the Jewish People (Judah, Benjamin and most of Levy) will share in the World-to-Come, but rather all Israelites. Certainly, according to R. Akiva, the Ten Tribes are excluded from this glorious future.

How one can reconcile R. Akiva's negative position towards the return of the Ten Tribes with the descriptions of the Prophet Ezekiel? In great detail, the latter predicted the reunification of the whole House of Israel, the advent of the Messiah, King of Israel, and the restoration of the glorious Kingdom of David, as well as described the division of the Land of Israel among the Twelve

Tribes (Ezekiel 37:15-28; 47:13; 48:1-7 and 23-28). How can one reconcile R. Akiva's position with the strong assurances given by the prophet Jeremiah when he speaks of the future fate of the whole House of Israel: *"And I will cause the captivity of Judah and the captivity of Israel to return, and will build them, as at the first"* (Jer.33:7, emphasis mine).

Is it not self-evident that the Twelve Tribes will have to be present in the days of Moshiach (*"Yemot ha-Mashiach"*)? As we read in Amos, "And I will return My people Israel, and they will re-build desolate cities and dwell in them, and they will plant vineyards and drink their wine and plant gardens and eat their fruit. And I will plant them on their land, and they will not be removed again from the land that I have given to them, says Hashem your God" (9:15-16).

How is it possible to claim that Israel (i.e. the Ten Tribes) will perish and not return? Do we have a slightest doubt concerning God's Bible? How can we believe Rabbi Akiva and ignore the plain statements of our Creator? Why should we take the former's opinion on the subject of the Ten Tribes as truthful over the Sacred Word of the Almighty? The Scripture and the sages say that the Ten Tribes will eventually return to the Promised Land and receive the Heavenly Torah once more.

The ancient prophet from Pethor in Mesopotamia, Balaam, son of Beor, thus characterized the truthfulness of God of Israel: "God is not a man, that he should lie, nor a son of man, that he should change his mind. Does He speak and then not act? Does He promise and not fulfill" (Numbers 23:19)? The Ten Tribes of Israel have never been lost for Almighty God: *"Mine eyes are upon all their ways; they are not hid from My face"* (Jeremiah 16:17, emphasis mine). And later, God's commitment is reaffirmed: "Thus saith the LORD; If My covenant be not with day and night, and if I have not appointed the ordinances of heaven and earth; then will I cast away the seed of Jacob, and David my servant, so that I will not take any of his seed to be rulers over the seed of Abraham, Isaac, and Jacob: for I will cause their captivity to return, and have mercy on them" (Jer.33:25, 26).

What purpose could it serve for R. Akiva to use certain verses as evidence that the Ten Tribes will not come back to the Promised Land and have a part in the World-To-Come? Many verses (as we shall see) in other chapters of the Tanakh, Talmud, and Rabbinical Literature overwhelmingly say the opposite, as this passage attests: "I will gather them to their own land, not leaving any behind. I will no longer hide My Face from them, for I will pour out My Spirit on the house of Israel, declares the Sovereign HaShem" (Ezekiel 39:29). Talmudic tradition says, "It is forbidden to be amongst those who deny the redemption." We may add that this important opinion of the sages should include those who deny the Redemption of the 'lost' Ten Tribes of Israel.

CHAPTER I

Bar Kokhba

The Character of Bar Kokhba

There are intimations in rabbinical sources of the larger-than-life personality traits of Bar Kokhba. The military leader of the Jewish Revolt against the Roman Empire, he was known as a man of tremendous physical strength, with the ability to uproot a tree while riding a horse, or to haul back the stone thrown by a Roman catapult. The Talmud tells, for example, of his almost superhuman physical and military exploits: "And what did Bar Kokhba use to do? On one of his legs, he used to catch the ballista-balls fired from the enemy's catapults and throw them back, killing many men" (Lamentation Rabbah 2:2). His legendary personality has given rise to many controversial opinions. Some scholars have highly praised him as a national hero, glorious military commander, and freedom fighter who died for the freedom and independence of Judea in the course of the battle against the Roman Empire. They have valorized him as a hero-saint.

Bar Kokhba's legacy of a freedom fighter and as a national heroic leader has penetrated modern Jewish religious and secular society. It was especially manifested in the Betar movement, an early revisionist Zionist youth movement founded by Vladimir Jabotinsky in early 1920s. Many prominent politicians in Israel, including former Prime Ministers Yitzhak Shamir and Menachem Begin were members of this organization. During WWII, Betar served as a major provider of Jewish fighters against the Nazis in Europe and the British in Palestine. Today, the Betar Movement is still strong and active, promoting and disseminating ideals of patriotism, freedom, and Jewish leadership on university campuses, middle-schools, and in local communities.

Of the many legends about Bar Kokhba in Jewish literature, one is particularly fascinating. According to the tale, Bar Kokhba and the a lion, the king of the beasts, met in the Judean Mountains and engaged in fierce struggle that ended with the total subjugation of the wild animal by Bar Kokhba's supernatural strength. Animosity was followed by friendship. Legend says that people often saw Bar Kokhba riding on the lion in the twilight of the Judean wilderness. Legend also says that Bar Kokhba and the lion were captured by the Romans and brought to Rome. The Romans planned to entertain the public with a single combat to the death between a deliberately starved fierce lion and Bar Kokhba. During the fight Bar Kokhba again subordinated the lion that recognized its old friend. Then Bar Kokhba jumped on the lion's back and they escaped the Coliseum arena to join his Judean freedom-fighting comrades in the rebellion against the Romans. As the words in the folk song translate,

> *"Over mountains and valleys he cruised, raising the banner of liberty. The whole nation applauded him: Bar Kokhba, hurrah!"*

The lion fought side by side with Bar Kokhba in the war against the Romans. One day, the lion was mortally wounded. Bar Kokhba stopped the fight and bended over his dying friend to pet him one last time. At that very moment the Roman's arrow fatally hit him and he fell, embracing the lion as he lay beside him. Thus concludes the legend of the life and death of the Jewish hero and the king lion (Levin Kipnis, "Bar Kokhba and the lion").

Despite the power of the legend, many researches think of Bar Kokhba as an imposter claiming to be the Messiah, a reckless thug, a brutal, arrogant, and godless dictator, a worthless shepherd, and an irresponsible leader of a nation, who brought many woes and much misfortune and destruction to the Jewish people. Whereas one source presents him as a charismatic, highly intelligent personality, faithful to God and obedient to the Laws of the Torah, from another source he emerges as a self-confident and decisive but temperamental leader.

Together with his magnetic personality, his initial, considerable military success on battlefield against the Romans, has attracted many rabbis and scholars, among them R. Akiva. The people of Judaea also accepted him with all their heart and soul as the natural leader of the revolt against the Romans. It was hoped that he would lead them to liberty and independence, as well as restore Israel to its glorious past.

On the other hand, as revealed in the Talmud, Bar Kokhba had not justfied hopes and expectations as the God's sent Messiah. Thus, during the organization of the army of freedom fighters, Bar Kokhba required any man who wished to join to cut off his little finger as a token of devotion to the cause of the Revolt and a sign of personal strength and bravery. It was, however, in direct contradiction to the Law of Torah which prohibits self-mutilation. On this account, the rabbis objected to the practice, asking, "How long will you continue to mutilate Israel?" Bar Kokhba answered, "How else is it possible to test them?" They said to him, "Anyone who cannot uproot a cedar of Lebanon while riding on his horse shall not be enlisted in your army." So he had 200,000 of the former and 200,000 of the latter (i.e. 200,000 fighters with amputated fingers and 200,000 with the physical ability to uproot a cedar tree while riding a horse). It is of interest to note that the rabbis opposed only the practice of violating the Halakhah, not the war against the Romans. The sages of the Sanhedrin and the Academy of Yavneh had fully supported Bar Kokhba as the Messiah and his military Revolt against the Roman Empire.

Bar Kokhba's cruelty did not end there. The Talmudic story reveals that Bar Kokhba was not only a brutal dictator but also a cruel man and murderer. In the city of Bethar, the headquarters of Bar Kokhba's army where the Sanhedrin and the majority of the sages of the Academy of Yavneh had found a safe haven under protection of the rebels, a Samaritan falsely accused Rabbi Eleazar of conspiring to surrender the city of Bethar to the Romans. Bar Koknba unjustly killed his old uncle, the righteous Rabbi Eleazar of Modiin, the disciple of Johanan ben Zakkai, whose wisdom had been recorded in the Talmud:

"Rabbi Elazar of Modiin said: 'One who profanes sacred things, and one who despises the festivals, and one who causes his fellow's face to blush in public, and one who annuls the covenant of our father Abraham, may he rest in peace, and he who is contemptuous towards the Torah, even though he has to his credit [knowledge of the] Torah and good deeds, he has not a share in the World to Come'" (Avot 3:11).

Rabbi Eleazar happened to be one of the wise men of Israel who had opposed the military revolt against the Romans. He had not accepted Bar Kokhba as the prophesied Jewish Messiah. Some scholars speculate that it is he who appears as Eleazar the High Priest on the Bar Kokhba coins of the Second Jewish-Roman War (132-135 CE). Because of his prayers that God "should not sit in judgment today," the Romans did not capture the city of Bethar. Prayer, not the might of Bar Kokhba's army, prevailed. That is why Scripture calls R. Eleazar, who trusted in God, "the arm of all Israel." Bar Kokhba, who rejected the power of God and relied on his own power and the military strength of his army, is deemed "a worthless shepherd" (Midrash Rabbah, Lamentations 2.2&4).

As soon as Bar Kokhba killed R. Eleazar, a voice from heaven issued forth and proclaimed, "Woe to the worthless shepherd that leaves the flock! The sword shall be upon his arm, and upon his right eye" (referring to Zechariah 11:17). On that same day, August 9, 135 CE, the Romans attacked and breached the walls of Bethar. They killed Bar Kokhba and massacred virtually the entire population of the city. The city of Betar was the last rebel stronghold to resist Roman conquest. The Talmud explains that the sins of the people caused Bethar to be captured. Men, women, and children were slain. Small children and infants were picked up by their feet and their heads dashed against large rocks. The Midrash claims that on a single large rock three hundred infants were killed by such grotesque means, so that it became covered with the evidence of savage customs. It was also said that the Roman legionaries wrapped Jewish infants in Torah scrolls—the Jews' sacred texts—and burned them alive. When the Roman Calvary crossed the river of the city on horseback during the assault, their horses waded up to their nostrils in the blood-red water. The slaughter of the Jews was so massive that Talmud reports that, "It was taught that for seven years the gentiles cultivated their vineyards with the blood of Israel without requiring manure for fertilization" (Gittim 57a).

As a matter of fact, the first genocidal Holocaust in Jewish history happened not during World War II in the time of Hitler but two thousand years beforehand in the time of Emperor Hadrian, during the suppression of the Bar Kokhba Revolt. Almost one million Jews of Judaea were wiped out by the Roman sword without mercy in a manner reminiscent of the Nazi atrocities during the Final Solution.

When Bar Kokhba's head was brought to Hadrian, he asked, "Who killed him?" A Samaritan answered, "I killed him." "Bring his body to me," ordered the Emperor. When he saw the body with a snake encircling his neck, Hadrian exclaimed, "If his God had not slain him, who could have overcome him?" As it is written, 'Unless their Rock had sold them, and the Lord had surrendered them'" (Deuteronomy 32:30; Jerusalem Talmud Ta'anit 4:5, Midrash Rabbah-Eicha 2:4). In the Rabbinical tradition, death caused by snakes demonstrates divine retribution to a sinful person. In the case of Bar Kokhba, tradition dictates that he was not killed by the Romans but by God (Gen. Rab. 44.21; Exodus Rabbah 51.7; Pesachim Rabbah 30.3).

There is another story in the Talmud describing the death of Bar Kokhba at the hands of the rabbis: "Bar Koziba reigned two and a half years, and then said to the Rabbis, "I am the Messiah." They answered, "Of the Messiah it is written that he smells and judges (referring to Isaiah 11:2-4); let us see whether he [Bar Koziba] can do so. When they saw that he was unable to judge by the scent, they slew him" (Talmud, Sanhedrin 93b).

This strange and puzzling account testifies that Bar Kokhba indeed called himself the Messiah; it also goes against the well-established historical fact that Bar Kokhba was killed by the Romans, not the rabbis. Further, the name of R. Akiva is not mentioned in connection with Bar Kokhba the Messiah. Was the account not an earlier attempt to minimize or even hide the great mistake and embarrassment to Rabbinical Judaism that this renowned sage caused by proclaiming the wrong man to be the God-chosen Messiah? This rabbinical text most likely presents an anecdote or legend rather than historical evidence.

Was Bar Kokhba The Messiah?

Did Bar Kokhba consider himself the Messiah? We think he did. Besides the confirmation of this fact in the Talmudic source material, there are other indications available. In an interesting story recorded by Jerome (c. 340-420AC) Bar Kokhba performed all kind of ostensibly miraculous acts in a determined effort to gain the title of Messiah: "That famed Barchochebas, [Ben Koziba], the instigator of the Jewish uprising, kept fanning a lighted blade of straw in his mouth with puffs of breath so as to give the impression that he was spewing out flames" (Jerome, Against Rufinus 3.31). This kind of miracle, according to some Talmudic traditions, was performed by Bar Kokhba in an attempt to be recognized as the legitimate Messiah: "Behold, when he saw the onrush of the approaching multitude, he neither lifted his hand nor held a spear or any weapon of war; but I saw how he sent forth from his mouth as it were a stream of fire, and from his lips a flaming breath, and from his tongue he shot forth a storm of sparks. All these were mingled together, the stream of fire and the flaming breath and the great storm, and fell on the onrushing multitude which was prepared to fight, and burnt them all up, so that suddenly nothing was seen of the innumerable multitude but only the dust of ashes and the smell of smoke" (4 Ezra 13.9-11).

Such strident efforts were evidently successful, as Maimonides describes Bar Kokhba as "a great king whom all of Israel, including the great sages, were convinced was the messiah" (Hilchot Ta'aniot Ch. 5, Hilchot Melachim Ch. 11). In his church history, Eusebius (260-339CE) records that "At that time a certain Bar Chochebas by name, which means 'star,' was the general of the Jews, who among other characteristics was a cut-throat and a bandit, but who relied on his name, as if dealing with slaves, and boasted that he was a star that had come down from heaven to shed light upon them in their misery" (4.1 Eusebius, *Ecclesiastical History*, 4: 6).

Since R. Akiva clearly declared Simon ben Koziba the Jewish Messiah—"This is the King Messiah!" (Midrash Rabbah, Lamentations 2.2&4)—and sealed his decision with the prophecy of "a star [that] goes forth from Jacob" (Numbers 24:17), it would seem that Bar Koziba had been transformed from a name connoting 'son of the lie' or 'son of the disappointment' into Bar Kokhba, 'son of the star,' the Messiah son of David. In sharp contrast to Jerome, Eusebius, and the other historical authorities, R. Akiva's perception of Bar Kokhba the Messiah was not associated with divine miracles and supernatural actions. According to Oppenheimer, in making his historical announcement R. Akiva emphasized the word "king" rather than "messiah," expecting the General Bar Kokhba earthly actions (in the manner of King David)—that is, the liberation of the Jewish people, the establishment of Judean independence, the rebuilding of the Temple, and the bringing of the Messianic Era to the nations of the World. By proclaiming Bar Kokhba the Messiah, R. Akiva breached the very important principle of Judaism that the arrival of the Messiah is not dependent solely on humans or anything other than the will of God, who alone shall decide the time of revelation.

The origins of Bar Kokhba's name are significant, and tell a tale of deceit and corruption. In a Midrash called "Rabbi," attributed to R. Judah *Ha-Nasi*, the name 'Koziva' is connected with the word '*kazav*,' meaning falsehood. According to R. Yohanan, "Rabbi would expound, 'A star shall step forth from Jacob' thus: do not read 'star' [*kokhav*] but 'liar' [*kozav*]." In other words, R. Judah Ha-Nasi saw Bar Kokhba not as a conquering messianic star arising out of Jacob but as a liar and a false messiah, in keeping with the prophesy from Numbers 24:17. The important message here is that Bar Kokhba failed not because redemption is impossible but because he was a worthless impostor of the real Messiah.

Bar Kokhba indeed regarded himself as the Messiah, as the rising star from Jacob to whom Balaam's prophecy applied. His inflated self-image can be amply seen from the images and Paleo-Hebrew descriptions on the coins that he struck during his two and a half years rule over the newly re-established independent state of Judea. On most of the coins the name 'Shimon' appears, likely referring to the leader of the Revolt, Simon Bar Kokhba.

He ruled with the title of *Nasi,* meaning 'Prince' in Hebrew—a common synonym for Messiah. (See Ezekiel 37:25: "My servant David shall be their Prince forever"). The Qumran eschatological literature also associates *Nasi* with the Messianic expectation of the heroic warrior who will defeat the hated Romans and restore the glorious Davidic Kingdom of justice and peace.

On the obverse side of the coins are depicted images of the Jewish Temple with the Ark of the Covenant inside of it and a rising star above the Temple, surrounded by the name 'Shimon, Prince of Israel.' The image of a star above the Temple appeared on many coins, probably in reference to Bar Kokhba's nickname 'Son of the Star.' On the reverse side of the coins are Hebrew inscriptions: *'One year of the Redemption of Israel,' 'For the freedom of Jerusalem,'* or *'Year two of the Freedom of Israel.'* The word 'redemption' in Judaism is often associated with the arrival of the Messiah and the future Messianic liberation and deliverance of the whole House of Israel. The depiction of the images of the Temple and the Ark of the Covenant on Bar Kokhba Revolt coinage indicates that the rebuilding of the Temple was one of the priorities of R. Akiva and Bar Kokhba. Some scholars have suggested that Bar Kokhba, in order to prove that he was the true Messiah, and under the instructions of R. Akiva, actually rebuilt the holy Temple in Jerusalem during the years of the Revolt. They refer to a Midrash (Exodus Rabbah 51:5) in which it is purportedly said that Hadrian entered the Holy of Holies of the Third temple. They also cite a passage from the Sibylline Oracles and the seventh-century Byzantine historian Chronicum Paschale, who in his history of the Jews wrote: "Hadrian tore down the Temple of the Jews in Jerusalem," indicating Bar Kokhba's construction of the Temple. Even the depiction of the Temple on the Bar Kokhba coins, they say, may be taken as evidence that the Temple existed. Otherwise, they argue, it would make no sense for the Jews to show images of the Temple on these coins.

All of this testifies to the fact that Bar Kokhba had considered himself the Messiah. In addition to this, according to one of the most important archeological discoveries of recent times, in the letters of Bar Kokhba found in the Cave of Letters in the Dead Sea area, written in Bar Kokhba's own hand and addressed to his fellows rebels, he frequently starts and ends with the same wording, 'Simeon, son of Kosiba, the ruler over Israel, to Jonathan and Masabala, peace!' or 'On the twenty-eight marhesvan of the third year of Simon ben Koziba, prince of Israel.'

Some Talmudic and Rabbinical sources point out that the Roman Authorities disqualified the Bar Kokhba coins as 'false Jerusalem coins' or 'danger money' after suppressing the Jewish Revolt. It was forbidden to possess or use them under the threat of severe punishment. The Romans did everything they could to erase the memory of the Bar Kokhba Revolt.

The fact that the Romans managed to defeat the 350,000 to 400,000 fighters of the Bar Kokhba army with a mere 80,000 to 120,000 troops (a total force of 12 legions) speaks for itself. Just at the battle of Bethar alone, as the Midrash says, "Eighty thousand trumpeters besieged Bethar where Bar Kozeba was located, who had with him two hundred thousand men with an amputated finger" (Rabbah Lamentations 2:4). Ironically, the Emperor Hadrian, the bloody prosecutor of the Jewish people, drank himself to death on July 10, 138 CE, just three years after the Bar Kokhba Revolt. The death of Hadrian was a significant relief for the surviving Jewish communities. His successor, Emperor Antonius Pius (138-161 CE) was a good, peaceful man who promoted arts and sciences, and built temples, theaters, and mausoleums. His style of government was highly praised by his contemporaries and by later generations.

In stark contrast, Bar Kokhba had not been a man of God. He had relied on his own pride and power, and demonstrated arrogance in spiritual matters. He managed to assemble a 350,000 to 400,000 strong army of fighters against the total force of twelve

Roman legions, who numbered 80,000 to 120,000 soldiers. Despite this, he lost the war because he was an illegitimate Messiah and the war was not according to the will of God. When he led his army to battle, the rabbis would bless the soldiers saying, "May the God of Israel help them." They were acting precisely as if it was a war sanctioned by God Himself, a description of which we find in Scripture:

"When you go out to battle against your enemies, and see horses and chariots and people more numerous than you, do not be afraid of them; for the Lord your God is with you, who brought you up from the land of Egypt. So it shall be, when you are on the verge of battle that the priest shall approach and speak to the people. And he shall say to them, Hear, O Israel: Today you are on the verge of battle with your enemies. Do not let your heart faint, do not be afraid, and do not tremble or be terrified because of them; for the Lord your God is He who goes with you, to fight for you against your enemies, to save you" (Deuteronomy 20:1-4). This is what we call 'The War of God!' There are many examples in Scripture of God's victorious involvement in battles on the side of His People of Israel (Exodus 14:13, 14, 25; Deuteronomy 1:30; 3:22; Joshua 10:11-14, 25,42; 23:3, 10; 1 Samuel 17:47; 2 Chronicles 20:17, 29; 32:7-8; Psalms 35:1; Jeremiah 1:19; 15:20-21). The Scripture calls these wars 'holy' because they are defined as wars fought on behalf of the people of Israel either by or on the authority of the God of Israel.

To the blessings of the rabbis, the rebels of Bar Kokhba would answer that, "God can neither be of value nor of harm. He will not assist nor weaken." This gross denial of the authority of the Almighty and His Divine Power partly explains the outcome of the war. Before he commenced battle against the Romans, Bar Kokhba is said to have claimed: "O Lord God of Hosts, does not stand at our right hand, nor be against us, for You, O God, have abandoned us. We ourselves shall be victorious over the enemy."

How could he say, "God, You need not bother to help us. Just do not help our enemies"? Clearly no Messiah ordained by God would speak in such a manner. In the Jerusalem Talmud there are comments that Bar Kokhba kept repeating the verse from Psalms 60:12: "You have rejected us, O God; God, You do not march with our armies."

The historian Eusebius wrote that Bar Kokhba persecuted the Christians and killed them if they refused to help him fight against the Roman troops. Justin Martyr (c.100-165 CE), the Christian apologist, makes precisely the same claim: "For in the present Jewish war it was only Christians whom Bar Chochebas, the leader of the rebellion of the Jews, commanded to be punished severely, if they did not deny Jesus as the Messiah and blaspheme him." Almost all of the Christians at that time were Jews. How could they possibly join Bar Kokhba the Messiah if they were expecting the imminent return of their own Messiah, Jesus Christ?

This is the man (Bar Kokhba) who R. Akiva called the King Messiah. Recall that the original name of Bar Kokhba is said to have been Simon *Bar Kozeba,* which in Hebrew means, 'Son of lies' or 'Son of deception.' As we know, R. Akiva changed the original name to Bar Kokhba. The meaning of Kokhba is 'a star' and R. Akiva attributed the new name to a messianic prophecy: "A Star shall come out of Jacob" (Numbers 24:17). In contrast, here is the portrait of the future Messiah provided by the sages: "He is free from sin, from desire for wealth or power, a pure, wise, and holy King imbued with the spirit of God, he will lead all to righteousness and holiness" (Rabbah Cant.17: 32-43; Midrash Teh.72:12; Targum Yer. To Genesis 44:12; Isaiah 11:2; 41:1).

The name change could not, and did not, transform a man whose morals and values were in no way a reflection of the Scriptural character of the Messiah as it has been prophesied throughout the ages.

The Failure of the Bar Kokhba Revolt and Its Consequences

Indeed, the God of Israel was not with Bar Kokhba, R. Akiva, his multitude of disciples, or the majority of the Judeans who had been seduced and enticed by their leaders to take part in a doomed uprising against the Romans. Most of them paid the ultimate price for their actions with their lives. The main reasons for their catastrophic defeat, from the perspective of Scripture, are as follows. The God of Israel was not with the rebels because it was not a Holy War. The 'lost' Ten Tribes had not been found. That generation of Judeans did not repent of their sins, and therefore did not merit redemption. Bar Kokhba was not chosen by God as the Messiah son of David, the anointed King of Israel. It was not the prophesized Messianic Time. In other words, the declaration of Bar Kokhba as Messiah was premature. It was ahead of the appointed time.

Similarly, a large number of Ephraimites, in the time of Moses before the Exodus from Egypt, miscalculated the time of the Deliverance by thirty years (1 Chronicles 7:20-21; Psalms 78:9). They attempted to leave and were killed by the Philistines. In both cases the events ended with a disastrous defeat and slaughter. In the earlier example of disobedience, the Israelites ignored and transgressed the direct command of God not to go to the Promised Land before the appointed time, so that Moses pleaded with them: "Why do you disobey the Lord's command? It will not succeed. Go not up, for the LORD is not among you; that you be not smitten before your enemies. But they presumed to go up to the hill top. Then the Amalekites came down, and the Canaanites who dwelt in that hill country, and struck and defeated them" (Numbers 14:40-45).

Not many realize what grave consequences the rebellion of Bar Kokhba (with the blessing of R. Akiva) had for the Jewish nation.

It was a catastrophic defeat in which 800,000 Jews killed, and 985 villages and 50 fortresses were demolished. The rest of the Jews were sold into slavery and exiled to the 'lands of their enemies.' The scholars of Judaea were executed, the sacred Torah scrolls burnt. The Torah was prohibited. Jerusalem was plowed in fulfillment of the prophecy in Micah 3:12, "Zion will be plowed like a field." The Jewish municipality of Jerusalem was replaced by the Roman pagan city of *Aelia Capitolina*. The names of 'Judaea' and 'Israel' were wiped out and the name *Syria Palaestina* substituted.

Here is how the Roman historian Dio Cassius described the situation aftermath of the crushed rebellion: "Thus nearly the whole of Judea was made desolate, a result of which the people had had forewarning before the war. For the tomb of Solomon, which the Jews regarded as an object of veneration, fell to pieces of itself and collapsed. And many wolves and hyenas rushed howling into the cities. Many Romans, however, perished in this war. Therefore, Hadrian, in writing to the Senate, did not employ the opening phrase commonly affected by emperors: 'If you and your children are in health it is well and I and my legions are in health.'"

Historians, theologians, rabbis, and authors have spoken of the Bar Kokhba Revolt 132-135 CE as the greatest tragedy in Jewish history. According to Rabbi Reuven Subar, "The destruction of Jerusalem can be called the Jewish tragedy extraordinaire. It claimed millions of lives and unleashed a 2,000 year torrent of crusades, pogroms, jihads and holocausts. Arguably, it is the worst thing that ever happened to the Jewish people. The death of the Torah's scholars alone is a global tragedy, because 'Torah scholars increase peace in the World" (Berachot 64a; Psalm 122).

The Emperor Hadrian realized that to eliminate the Jewish rebellious spirit it was not enough to kill most of the Jews. He would also need to destroy the foundation of their beliefs and strength—that is, Judaism itself. That is why, after crushing Bar Kokhba Revolt, the Emperor issued decrees that outlawed

Judaism. Violators were immediately sentenced to cruel death; Jews were forbidden to enter Jerusalem. Roman historian Eusebius of Caesarea confirms as much: "Jews were *thereafter* strictly forbidden even to set foot on the land around Jerusalem" (Eusebius, Ecclesiastical History iv.6, emphasis added).

From the statement of the Christian contemporary chronicler Aristo Pellaeus (100-160 CE) (attributed to him by Eusebius), it is evident that he agrees with the order of the events, "The whole nation *from that time* was strictly forbidden to set foot on the region about Jerusalem, by the formal decree and enactment of Hadrian, who commanded that they should not even from a distance look on their native soil" (emphasis mine). The language of these writings, particularly the words 'thereafter' or 'from that time,' imparts the sense that such narrative stories of exclusion emerged after the suppression of the Bar Kokhba rebellion.

Hadrian unleashed a reign of fearsome religious persecution that is unprecedented in the history of the Jewish nation. Two millennia of exile, and with it, unspeakable suffering began. The consequences of the failed rebellion of the House of Judah continue into the present. As Rabbi Pinchas Stolper writes, "Every anti-Semitic outbreak for which Jews suffered since that day of the tragic defeat, every pogrom, massacre, crusade, Holocaust, and banishment that took the toll of so many millions during the two thousand year long and bitter night of exile, wandering and persecution, must be traced directly to the failure of Bar Kochba— but ultimately to the failure of the students of Rabbi Akiva."

Others have echoed Stolper's sentiments, questioning the moral compass and judgment of the man who endorsed Bar Kokhba as the Messiah. Daniel Gruber directly points the finger at R. Akiva: "The disaster was compounded by the fact that R. Akiva, the father of rabbinic Judaism, proclaimed Bar Kokhba, the leader of the rebellion, to be God's Anointed, the Messiah." Franz Rosenzveig, a Jewish theologian and philosopher writing in the beginning of the last century, wondered, "Why did even the wisest teacher of his age fall for the false messiah, Bar Kokhba, in the time of Hadrian?"

The war was indisputably politico-Messianic in nature. The defeat of Bar Kochba marked the end of any sort of Jewish autonomy in the Jewish homeland until the twentieth century. What we know for certain is that a spiritual leader of the caliber of R. Akiva together with the respected sages of the Sanhedrin and the Academy of Yavneh could have prevented (instead of exacerbating) the tragic results of the Bar Kokhba Revolt. They had an enormous influence and authority among the extremely religious Jewish population of Judaea. Without their support, as an *Avodah* post says, "The revolt's apparent organizational and logistical success would not have been possible."

There is, however, a famous saying of R. Akiva, "Everything Hashem does is for the good. *Gam zu l'tovah.* Didn't I tell you that everything that Hashem does is for the best?" (Gomoro Brochos 60b). Evidently the tragic mistake of designating the wrong man to be the God-chosen Messiah, his failure in predicting the Messianic Times, and the grave consequences for the Jewish people resulting from him with initiating and spiritually leading the Bar Kokhba Revolt—all of this has not seemingly harmed the reputation of R. Akiva as the great sage in Judaism. Who knows how the course of Jewish (and the world) history would have gone if the catastrophic Bar Kokhba Revolt had been prevented?

CHAPTER II

The Bar Kokhba Revolt and Rabbi Akiva

Was the Revolt Caused by the Roman Ban on Circumcision?

The Bar Kokhba Revolt (132-135 CE) did not start spontaneously and unexpectedly. It is not a secret that Emperor Hadrian and his administration, in fact, accelerated the revolt through a whole range of irresponsible actions—by sanctioning the cruelty of the governor of Judea Quintus Tineius Rufus; by planning to build a temple dedicated to Jupiter on the very site of the Second Temple; and by planning to build the new city and issuing the Roman coin in 132 CE (doubtfully) inscribed with the words 'Aelia Capitolina' instead of 'Jerusalem.' The Judeans hated the Roman occupiers, and any act of aggravated cruelty, significant religious persecution, or perceived insult to the God of Israel may have sparked a rebellion, as explicitly related in the Midrash (Bereshit Rabbah, 64).

Cassius Dio states in the *Historia Romana* that the cause of the Bar Kokhba revolt was Hadrian's construction of Aelia Capitolina on the site of Jerusalem and the construction of a temple to Jupiter on the Temple mount. It may have been that the Jews, out of fear of losing their beloved Jerusalem and the holy Temple, revolted against the Romans. There are a few historians who contend that the cause of the Bar Kokhba Revolt was the Roman edict forbidding circumcision. Thus, an ancient source, the *History of Augusta*, a collection of biographies of Roman emperors, states: "At this time also the Jews began a war, because they were forbidden to mutilate their genitals" (*Vita Hadriani* 14.2).

It is unrealistic to think that Emperor Hadrian would have undertaken such decisive actions against the Jews. He knew the deep-seated hostility between the Romans and Jews. It was not in Rome's interests to provoke a new bloody war with the Jews. Various draconian measures had been taken in the aftermath of the defeat of the Bar Kokhba rebellion as punishment to the Jewish nation for their uprising: Rome had changed the name of Judaea to Provincia Syria Palaestina, prohibited the Jews from living in Jerusalem and resettled it with foreign inhabitants, built the Roman city Aelia Capitolina instead of the Jewish ancient capital, constructed the temple of Zeus on the very spot where the Solomon Temple stood (i.e. on the Temple Mount), and forbidden the practice of Judaism, including circumcision.

Some argue that there was no Roman edict whatsoever prohibiting circumcision of the Jews before the Revolt. However, there was Roman legislation concerning the castration of male slaves in connection with the ever-growing eunuch business. Castration was defined as bodily mutilation, and is clearly completely different in practice and principle from Jewish circumcision. There is a world of difference between the Roman law of castration and the religious ban on circumcision. The castration edict was not directed against the religious circumcision of the Jews—at least, that was not the case before the Bar Kokhba Revolt. There was another piece of Roman legislation directed against converts to Judaism, prohibiting them from being circumcised. This law was in line with the official Roman policy against proselytism. There is not one single document or any other source confirming that the Romans had a law forbidding circumcision for the Jews before the Bar Kokhba Revolt.

The ritual of circumcision is a foundation of Judaism, the direct command of God to His People Israel: "This is My covenant, which you shall keep, between Me and you and your seed after you: Every male among you shall be circumcised" (Genesis 17:10). This commandment is incumbent upon both father and child. Here is the blessing recited by the father of the child about to be circumcised, "Blessed are You, Lord our God, Ruler of the Universe, who has sanctified us with Your commandments and commanded us to bring him into the covenant of Abraham, our father."

Any religious Torah-observant Jew dies rather than disobeys the commandment of circumcision. It does not matter whether the Emperor Hadrian liked or disliked the Jews. He knew the recent history of the Maccabees and the Greeks, the First Great Jewish Revolt, and was sufficiently educated to realize that a decree prohibiting circumcision would undermine the peace in Judea and bring about open confrontation with the Jews. The Romans did not want another exhausted war with the Jews. They were, more or less, tolerant of the religions of the conquered nations and concentrated mainly upon upholding the Roman laws, maintaining the political stability of the Empire, and levying collection taxes. We can therefore conclude that there was no Roman law prohibiting religious circumcision for the Jews before the Revolt. The cause of the Bar Kokhba Revolt should be searched for elsewhere.

The Building of the Pagan Temple in Jerusalem and the Revolt

Some people may say that Hadrian retracted his promise to the Jews to build them a Temple and, instead, built a pagan temple dedicated to Jupiter Capitolinus on the very spot where the Second Temple stood. The Talmudic sources point out that Hadrian's failure to build the Jewish Temple lies in the subversions of the Samaritans, who complained to the Emperor: "Be it known now unto the king, that, if this rebellious city be built and the walls finished, they will not pay tribute" (Midrash Genesis Rabbah, 64:29). Others say that it was the influence of the celebrated Roman historian Tacitus and his intellectual followers, who viewed themselves as the descendants of Greek culture and actively disseminated hatred against the Jews, who stood in the way of the temple's construction. Whoever it was, the Emperor abruptly changed his position from allowing the Jews to build their Temple to erecting a pagan temple dedicated to a Roman god on the site of the Jewish Temple. Many historians are of the opinion that the change in position was the real reason for the Bar Kokhba Revolt.

But was this reason sufficient justification for initiating the rebellion against mighty Rome? The Jews had been without the Temple and its sacrificial system for sixty years since its destruction by the Roman general Titus in 70 AC—punishment from God to a sinful nation. Had Judaism perished as a result of it? On the contrary, it adapted to the new circumstances and survived. R. Yohanan ben Zakkai said that the Jewish people could survive without the Holy Temple and its sacrificial system. As we read in the Scriptures, "For I desire mercy, and not sacrifice; and the knowledge of God more than burnt offerings" (Hosea 6:6), and "To do what is right and just is more acceptable to the LORD than sacrifice" (Proverbs 21:3). While Hadrian's decision to build a pagan Temple would have irritated Jews who must have felt betrayed and insulted, it still could not have been a decisive cause of mortal battle against the mighty Roman Empire.

There are some authors who suggest that the cause of the Bar Kokhba revolt was not the prohibition of circumcision or the founding of Aelia Capitolina or the building of the pagan temple in Jerusalem, but the decisions of its leader, Bar Kokhba. They validate their conclusion with the historical fact that Emperor

Hadrian visited the eastern provinces (including Land of Israel) in 129-130 CE. What did Hadrian's visit to Palestine have to do with the Bar Kokhba Revolt? Everything, they explain, because the visits of the Caesar, accompanied by building and development enterprises, imposed a heavy strain on the inhabitants of the Land of Israel who were forced, among other things, to cover the expenses of the emperor's royal retinue, as was the accepted practice. Bar Kokhba manipulated the wide-spread dissatisfaction of Judeans under Roman subjugation, and as soon as Hadrian left the region, he started armed Revolt.

These scholars, in searching for the true cause of the Bar Kokhba Revolt, have raised all kind of potential reasons for its emergence, but in doing so, they have missed the crucial one: R. Akiva's proclamation of Bar Kokhba as the God-sent Jewish Messiah. The dramatic announcement of the most respected religious teacher and spiritual leader of Israel served as decisive factor in mobilizing the masses of Judea in rebellion against the Roman Empire. During a time when Palestine brimmed with Messianic expectations, R. Akiva, considered by most to be a great and trusted leader of the nation, revealed to the Jews that God had finally sent the long-awaited Messiah in the person of the brave and strong General Bar Kokhba. And then, nothing could hold back or subdue the pressure of the Jewish people's anger and indignation against the Romans. In the minds and hearts of the people of Judea, the arrival of the Messiah was associated with the time of liberation, victorious Messianic wars, and redemption. That is why the majority of the Jewish population of Judea, including the sages of the Sanhedrin and the Academy of Yavneh, took an active part in the military uprising against hated Rome which ended in disastrous massacre, two thousand years of exile, and unparalleled persecution of the Jews. *R. Akiva's mistaken announcement of the wrong messiah is the main cause of the Bar Kokhba Revolt.*

Importantly, Eusebius Pamphili, bishop of Caesarea in Palestine, writing in the first quarter of the fourth century, says that *the building of the Roman temple in Jerusalem was a result of the Revolt, rather than a cause of it.* His assertion suggests that the Romans built the temple dedicated to Jupiter in Jerusalem in the aftermath of the suppression of the Bar Kokhba rebellion. Speaking of the foundation of Aelia Capitolina, Eusebius expressed the same opinion: "Thus, when the city had come to be free of the nation of the Jews, and its ancient inhabitants had been entirely destroyed, it was colonized by a foreign race and the Roman city that thereafter arose changed its name and was called Aelia in honor of the reigning emperor, Aelius Hadrian" (Eusebius, *The Ecclesiastical History* IV, 6).

In addition to his comprehensive description of historical events, Eusebius provided a clear chronology of the Bar Kokhba Revolt in his *Church History* and *Chronicle.* "In the Hadrian's Year 19, CE 134," he wrote, "The Jewish War that was conducted in Palestine reached its conclusion, all Jewish problems having been completely suppressed. From that time, the permission was denied them even to enter Jerusalem; first and foremost because of the commandment of God, as the prophets had prophesied; and secondly by authority of the interdictions of the Romans. In Hadrian's Year 20, CE 136, Aelia was founded by Aelius Hadrianus; and before its gate, that of the road by which we go to Bethlehem, he set up an idol of a pig in marble, signifying the subjugation of the Jews to Roman authority." As another consequence of this war, Jews were prohibited from living in the holy city, and the Romans issued Imperial decrees forbidding the practice of Judaism. *It is important to note that the Emperor Hadrian issued these religious prohibition laws, including the ban on circumcision, only after his victory over the rebels. All available sources testify to this fact.*

The Maccabees, the First Great Jewish Revolt, and the Bar Kokhba Rebellion: Reasons for the Jewish Uprisings

If we compare the historical situation in the time of the Maccabees to that of the Bar Kokhba Revolt, we see that the causes of the rebellions are fundamentally different. During the years of the Maccabees, the Seleucid Greek Emperor Antiochus IV Epiphanes (c.215-164 BCE), in his zealous pursuit of Alexander the Great's policy of Hellenization, decided to exterminate Judaism once and for all. He banned sacrifices, Sabbaths, feasts, and circumcision. Possession of the Torah was forbidden. Many sacred texts were burnt. All Jewish religious practices inherited from the time of Moses were forbidden by the decrees of Antiochus. Violators of these prohibitions were put to death. In the Holy Temple an idolatrous statue of Olympian Zeus was erected and unclean animals were sacrificed on the altar. All of these actions of the Greeks seriously threatened the long-established religion of the Jews and undermined their traditional way of life. The prohibition decrees were a direct assault against the Almighty God of Israel and His chosen people. The survival of Judaism and the Jewish nation itself was at stake. That is why the Jews rebelled against the Greeks and their draconian and idolatrous laws. That is why their uprising was legitimate from a Scriptural point of view. Their wars were 'holy wars' because the God of Israel was on their side. That is why the Maccabees were victorious and restored the independence of Judea and the freedom to worship the God of Israel and live by His Torah. And that is why, as the ultimate manifestation of divine approbation for the Maccabees, the miracle of Hanukkah happened.

In the cases of the First Great Jewish Revolt (66-70CE) and the Bar Kokhba Rebellion (132-135CE), the situation was markedly different. The Romans were more tolerant towards the religions of the conquered nations and did not impose religious prohibitions in the manner of the Greek Emperor Antiochus IV. Regrettably, there was one dramatic episode in Jewish history when, in 39CE, the reputedly insane Roman Emperor Caligula (reign 37-41CE), a self-absorbed epileptic and ruthless tyrant, declared himself a deity and ordered his statue to be erected in the Jerusalem Temple. The Jews refused to obey. They would have preferred to die than pollute God's Temple with idolatry. Caligula was angry and threatened to destroy the Temple if they disobeyed his order. The Jews sent a delegation to Rome in an attempt to pacify the Emperor and avoid bloody confrontation. The Emperor raged at them, "So you are the enemies of the gods, the only people who refuse to recognize my divinity." Luckily, Caligula was assassinated in 41CE at the age of 28 and bloody rebellion was prevented. The religious Jews had taken the death of the Emperor as a sign of divine retribution against all idolaters who fight against the God of Israel.

So, what were the established reasons for the first Great Jewish Revolt? Upon speculation, a whole range of possibilities present themselves: the Roman procurators of Judea were corrupted and cruel; the High Priests were Roman mercenary collaborators, appointed by and in service to, the Roman authorities rather than God and His people of Israel; the last procurator of Judea, Gessius Florus (64-66 CE), was notorious for his cruelty, public greed, and injustice to the Jewish population and Josephus Flavius credited him as being the primary cause of the Revolt (*Antiquities of the Jews*, Book 20, Chapter 11, Section 1). While all of these potential reasons are reasons enough, the *raison d'être* lies elsewhere.

First of all, it lies with the Jewish People themselves. It lies with their disunity, factional rivalry, causeless hatred, intolerance, and the religious fanaticism of the Zealots and Sicarii. When the Revolt started, it was they who brutally assassinated the Roman collaborators among the Jews, alongside all the moderate Jewish political and religious leaders of Judea, the Sadducees, Herodians, the wealthy elite, and idol worshippers. Basically, by using their preferred method of terrorist tactics, including kidnapping and assassination, the Sicarii ('dagger men') killed everyone who was opposed to the war against the Romans. They committed a series of atrocities against the civilian population in order to force the Jewish people to go to war with Rome. The destruction of the Second Temple and tragic defeat of the Jews in armed confrontation with the Roman Empire may not be attributable to the superiority of Rome but rather to the baseless hatred and fanatical rivalry of the Jewish factions.

The Role of the Messiah and Messianic Time in the Uprisings of the Jews

In our analysis of the causes of these three Jewish Revolts, it is important to determine the role that Jewish ideas concerning the Messiah and Messianic Time played in all of these events. In the course of the Maccabean wars there were a few prominent political and religious leaders such as Judah the Maccabee and his brother Jonathan who could have been recognized as Messiahs. In fact, they were accepted as kings and high priests, but never called themselves Messiah. The religious Jewish wise men of that time had understood the Scriptural teachings on the prophesied Messiah and the signs and conditions of the Messianic Age. The main source of historical information about the Maccabees and their wars, Books I and II of Maccabees, also confirms that no one individual had been called the Messiah during their rebellion. The goal of the Maccabees had been to fight against foreign oppressors and religious persecutors to achieve the independence of Judea and the freedom to worship the God of Israel. Though these are parallel goals to those of the Messiah (but limited in their scope), they did not depict their wars as Messianic wars or their times as the Messianic Times. Besides, the leaders of the Maccabees could not be recognized as Messiahs because they were not descendants of David. In addition, the restoration of the whole House of Israel, which is the most important task awaiting the Messiah, would not have been possible either in the time of the Maccabees, or during the three Jewish uprisings. The reasons for this conclusion have already outlined elsewhere on a few occasions.

The first Great Jewish Revolt did not reveal the leadership of the Messiah nor was its war against the Romans known as a Messianic war. These facts do not mean that the Messianic ideas were unknown to the Jews. Any time the Jewish nation suffers under foreign dominion, oppression, and religious persecution, its people cry and pray to the God of Israel to send them the Messiah, son of David, who will deliver them from all misfortune and bring about the Messianic era of freedom, love, and justice as promised in the words of His Prophets.

There was one occasion during the rebellion when Menahem ben Judah, the leader of the Sicarii, attempted to take over the leadership of the entire rebellion. He captured the Temple in Jerusalem and crowned himself as the Messiah-King. The population of Jerusalem was outraged. The captain of the Temple guards attacked and defeated the followers of Menahem. The newly proclaimed 'messiah' was apprehended, tortured, and executed.

As in the time of the Great Jewish Revolt, in the time of R. Akiva and the Bar Kokhba uprising there were many 'hot heads' among the Jews: religious fanatics, nationalistic patriots, zealots and all kind of extremists such as the Sicarii and other rascals, bandits, adventurers, and troublemakers who propagated and incited the masses to challenge Rome in armed rebellion. Josephus Flavius, who lived and wrote in the time of the first Great Jewish Revolt of 66 to 70AC, described in general the situation in Palestine thus: "Judea was now filled with bandits, and whoever found a few men to join with him in riots was set up as a king and they were hasty (to inflict) disaster on the people. They aggravated the Romans (but) a little, and a few (of them) murdered their own people" (*The Antiquities of the Jews*, book 17, chapter10). He explains the situation in greater detail elsewhere:

"Now when these were quieted, it happened, as it does in a diseased body, that another part was subject to an inflammation; for a company of deceivers and robbers got together, and persuaded the Jews to revolt, and exhorted them to assert their liberty, inflicting death on those that continued in obedience to the Roman government, and saying, that such as willingly chose slavery ought to be forced from such their desired inclinations; for they parted themselves into different bodies, and lay in wait up and down the country, and plundered the houses of the great men, and slew the men themselves, and set the villages on fire; and this till all Judea was filled with the effects of their madness. And thus the flame was every day more and more blown up, till it came to a direct war" (*The War of the Jews*, Book 2, chapter 13:6).

The religious and political leaders of Israel had also added oil to the fire. Most of the sages of the Sanhedrin and the Academy of Yavneh supported the Bar Kokhba Revolt. The spiritual leader of Israel, R. Akiva, not only pronounced the military commander Bar Kokhba as the Messiah, King of Israel, but went so far as to send his 24,000 students to join the army of rebels to fight against the Romans. The new generation of Judeans had already forgotten the bitter experience of the previous wars against the Roman Empire. The agitation of the stiff-necked nationalists, the terrorist acts of the stubborn religious zealots and the blessings of the rabbis, fanned the flames of war in their hearts and minds.

In the time of the first Great Jewish Revolt it was the criminal effort of the extremist Sicarii that, through intimidating terror, assassinations, and other tactics such as the destruction of food and water supplies, forced the Jews to fight against the Romans. *In the Bar Kokhba Revolt, the determining factor that mobilized and motivated the Jewish masses to war against Rome was the dramatic proclamation, issued by R. Akiva, that the military leader, Bar Kokhba, was the Messiah, son of David.* R. Akiva saw in Bar Kokhba the extraordinary, astonishing power of the Biblical *Gibborim*, a mighty, successful, and skillful warrior capable of defeating the ruthless Rome-Edom in final military battle. With this official revelation of the most renowned and respected sage of the time, nothing could stop the (mostly) religious population of Judea from joining the uprising under the flag of the Jewish Messiah, son of David. How could they possibly lose the war, if the Messiah was fighting for them? The proclamation of Bar Kokhba as the Messiah was the decisive turning point for a mass Jewish uprising that eventually led to devastating defeat and grave consequences for the Jewish people.

It is one thing to make a mistake in the interpretation of the laws of purity, kashrut or levirate regulation of family and marriage matters, or the rightful application of the *mitzvoth*, and quite another to enforce the Divine Timetable in choosing a Messiah of one's own design and calculate the Messianic Time without the approval of God. If the first mistakes are insignificant and can be easily corrected, the last mistake is of grand importance and engraved in the tragic fate of the Jewish nation of over 2,000 years of long horrific exile, millions of dead, and unparalleled sufferings and persecutions that can neither be forgiven nor forgotten.

No wonder that, according to Rabbi Michael Leo Samuel's blog post titled "Why did 24,000 students of R. Akiva die?," "Of all the explanations that seems to make the most amount of sense, Rabbi Akiba not only offered moral support to Bar Kochba, a man he believed to be the Messiah, he also encouraged his vast number of students to join in the apocalyptic battle against the Evil Empire of his day—Rome, as was first suggested by Rav Hai Gaon back in the 9th century C.E. The Romans regarded them much like we view Bin Laden and his fanatical terrorist organization Al Qaeda.

Roman leaders hunted the rabbis, especially Rabbi Akiba, since he was in their eyes the chief instigator of the Revolt" (emphasis mine).

Preparation for the Revolt and the Role of the Sages

The Jewish leaders had been covertly planning the revolt for more than fifteen years in an attempt to avoid the mistakes of the first Jewish Revolt fifty years earlier in 70 CE when Titus, the victorious Roman general, destroyed the Second Temple. The Jews built hideouts in caves, accumulated weapons, organized guerilla forces, and had been launching surprise attacks against the Romans for years (Dio Cassius, lxix. 12). Whereas in the previous uprising of 66 to 70 CE the Sanhedrin and the rabbis of Judaea had neither supported the rebels nor remained neutral, in the Bar Kokhba Revolt the majority of the sages of the Sanhedrin, the office of the *Nasi*, the Academy of Yavneh, and most of the rabbis actively welcomed and participated in the rebellion. They recognized messianic qualities in the personality of the national hero Bar Kokhba. After the widely respected spiritual leader of the Jewish nation, R. Akiva, proclaimed him to be the Messiah, anointed King of Israel, all the rabbis enthusiastically accepted him as the Messiah sent by God. The Talmudic stories mention that Bar Kokhba intended to free Jerusalem and establish the independence of Judaea. He was then going to build the Third Temple as proof that he was the Messiah according to Scripture but his efforts fell short due to Roman pressure and internal dissent.

Bar Kokhba was the military commander, organizer, and builder of the army of the freedom fighters. R. Akiva and his most prominent disciples were the spiritual-political leaders responsible primarily for the consolidation and unification of the rebels. They were also preoccupied with the collection of money and supplies, communication with the Diaspora, and the recruitment of new fighters from abroad. The rumors and expectations surrounding the ostensibly God-sent Messiah were such that, at this particular time in Judea, everyone believed that the coming revolt would be successful and that the Messianic Kingdom under the leadership of the Great Jewish Messiah Bar Kokhba was at hand.

Consider the situation before the Revolt as described in the *Jewish Encyclopedia*: "Even after R. Joshua ben Hanahiah succeeded in preventing the Jewish Revolt, the Jews remained quiet only on the surface; in reality, for over fifteen years they prepared for a struggle against Rome. The weapons that the Romans had ordered to be made by them they intentionally constructed poorly, so that they might keep them when rejected and returned to them. They converted the caves in the mountains into hiding-places and fortifications, which they connected by subterranean passages" (Dio Cassius, lxix. 12).

Although R. Akiva's role in the Jewish Revolt has not been precisely determined by historians (as the official version of Judaism maintains), there is much to suggest that he was actively involved as a religious and political leader of the Jewish nation. Since Judea had lost its independence and suffered humiliation in the First Jewish-Roman War (Great Jewish Revolt, 66-70 CE), there had not been a King or any other civilian authority for decades. The office of the *Nasi*, usually occupied by the rabbis, was a recognized religious and spiritual authority. The *Nasi* was also President of the Sanhedrin and acknowledged by the Romans as the patriarch of the Jews. This post had been empty since 120CE. Rabban Gamaliel II of Yavneh had held the title from 80 to 118CE followed by Rabbi Eliezar ben Azariah from 118CE to120CE. During the years of the Bar Kokhba Revolt the office of the *Nasi* remained vacant. R. Akiva, the wisest scholar of the Mishnah, with all his qualifications, should have had this office, but the sages constantly held back from voting to promote him to President of the Sanhedrin due to R. Akiva having come from a family of converts. From having been a poor, semi-literate shepherd, R. Akiva had progressed to become one of Judaism's greatest scholars. His lack of pedigree had, however, held him back from being appointed as the *Nasi*, leader of the Sanhedrin.

The people of Judea were looking to the rabbinical sages for spiritual guidance and direction in their everyday affairs. Generally, the Romans did not interfere in the internal life of subjected communities, as long as they were able to exercise full external political control of the provinces and collect taxes. The sages were respected and enjoyed privileges as leaders of the people. Of course, they did not have an army or police, but such forces were not necessary because people listened to them and voluntarily responded to their decisions as to the voice of God.

R. Akiva was heavily involved in preparations for the revolt because he was convinced that a military struggle against the Romans would finally bring victory to the Jews over their oppressors, liberate their nation, and establish an independent Kingdom of Judaea with its own King, the Messiah son of David. He was certainly not a peacemaker like his predecessor and teacher Rabbi Joshua. As the most influential spiritual leader of the nation, R. Akiva did not uphold the principle of teaching only what he learned from his teacher before him—a principle upheld by his own master, R. Eleazer ben Hyrcanus. All of his enormous knowledge and energy were directed to achieving liberty and independence for his people through armed struggle against a despised Rome.

R. Akiva and his contemporary sages had known the political situation in Palestine and were well aware of the mood and feelings of the Judeans. It was a unique time in the history of the Jewish people. Sad memories remained of the First Revolt— the destruction of the Second Temple and Jerusalem, followed by death, slavery and exile (66-70CE). There had also been a more recent war (110-118CE) against the Romans led by two brothers Pappius and Lulianus. This war too had ended in a bloody massacre of the Jews in the city of Lydd. All of these memories, contrary to Roman expectations, had not broken the will and spirit of the Judeans to continue their fight for freedom. When Pappius and Lulianus were asked by their Roman executioners, "Why does your God not save you as He did the three youths in Nebuchadnezzar's time?" they replied, "We are probably not worthy of such a miracle" (Ta'an. 18b). Immediately after this war, the Emperor Trajan was assassinated and succeeded by Hadrian.

Winds of hope for liberty and the restoration of the glorious past Kingdom of David and Solomon, for the building of the Third Temple, (which was promised by Emperor Hadrian), for the arrival of the Messiah, who would defeat their Roman oppressors and establish the glorious Kingdom of God in love and justice, had filled the hearts and minds of a new generation of Judeans. As in the wars and revolts of the past, there were many religious extremists and fanatics, radical fundamentalists, 'hot heads,' as well as zealots and terrorists with ever-present sectarian hatred and rivalry. Rumors of the imminent arrival of the Messiah and subsequent redemption were on the lips of every Jew. Judaea was literally a powder keg ready to explode at any moment.

Not all the rabbis were supportive of the Revolt against the Romans. It is of interest to know that the father of R. Shimon, Yochai, who was held in great esteem and respect among the Jewish people, was a peaceful man and a bitter opponent of the Revolt. As we shall see, R Yochai, R Eleazar from Modiin, and R. Yohanan ben Torta were not the only voices of dissent.

The Peacemaker R. Joshua ben Hanahiah

In rabbinical literature one finds many stories about Rabbi Joshua ben Hananiah, a leading sage of the Talmud and a key founder of Rabbinical Judaism. He had witnessed the destruction of the

Second Temple, along with the death of Jews and the humiliation of the Jewish nation resulting from the First Rebellion against the Romans in 66 to 70 CE. His teacher was the great Rabbi Johanan ben Zakkai who has been called 'The Father of Wisdom and the Father of Generations' [of Scholars]. After the death of Gamaliel II, Rabbi Joshua became President of the Rabbinical Council in the academy at Yavneh. In all his activities and decisions, he upheld the liberal views and principles of the school of Hillel and his teacher Johanan ben Zakkai from whom he had inherited tolerance and a love for peace. On a few occasions, when the politico-religious situation was ready to explode and the Jews were on the edge of revolt, Rabbi Joshua dissipated the people's anger and persuaded them to lay down their arms. This peaceful scholar was greatly respected even among his strongest opponents.

Why is it that in those turbulent times of political, social, and religious turmoil, R. Joshua ben Hananiah influenced religious zealots to pursue peace and avoid military confrontations with Rome (Gen. Rabbah lxix), whereas his student, R. Akiva, who after his death became the influential spiritual leader of the Jewish people, did not? In stark contrast to R. Joshua, R. Akiva was actively involved in politics, in the Bar Kokhba revolt (especially its preparation), and acknowledged the dictator and murderer Bar Kokhba as the Jewish Messiah. Where was Bar Kokhba's messianic spirit of wisdom and righteousness, when he did not even hide the fact that he did not trust in God but relied on his own power in the battle against the Romans, asserting that God will "neither assist nor discourage us?" Could such be the characteristic of the true Messiah? Or is it rather the character of a man the Talmud calls "Bar Koziba," meaning "the son of the liar?"

The wise men of the Talmud knew well what they were talking about when they wrote: *"Since Rabbi Joshua died (131CE), good counsel has ceased in Israel"* (Baraita, Sotah, end). They knew that a new generation of sages under the leadership of R. Akiva did not possess "good cancel," that is, the peacemaking abilities and loving kindness of R. Joshua who had loved and respected even his strongest opponents and was deservedly praised as a peacemaker not only among the Judeans but also the Romans.

It was R. Joshua who spoke to the Judaeans after Emperor Hadrian had reneged on his promise to rebuild God's Temple for the Jews in Jerusalem and planned to build a temple to Jupiter on the Temple Mount instead. A huge crowd had gathered, weeping and shouting in protest against the Romans. The people were on the verge of taking weapons in their hands and revolting when these words of R. Joshua pacified them:

"A lion while eating pray found that a bone had stuck in his throat. He roared out that whosoever would remove the bone out of his throat would be rewarded. A stork came and thrust his long bill into the lion's throat and drew forth the bone. The stork said, 'Give me my reward.' 'Your reward,' said the lion 'is that you will be able henceforth to boast that you are the only creature whose head was in the lion's mouth and came out alive.' "So it is with us," explained R. Joshua, "it is enough that we have emerged without harm from a decree by the Emperor."

In other words, the Jewish people ought to be satisfied with the fact that the Romans had allowed their return to the Holy Land after the disastrous events of the uprising of 66 to 70CE. The Jews, he concluded, ought to live in peace with the Romans and worship the God of Israel, who would look after them and restore them to their previous glory, when He would send the Messiah, son of David. And so it was that, as we read in the Midrash, "The Jews calmed down, laid their weapons aside and went to their homes" (Midrash Bereshit Rabbah, 64). In the opinion of the sages, Rabbi Joshua's peacemaking abilities among the people of Judaea were pivotal in preventing a third armed rebellion against the Roman Empire during the years of his life.

According to another story recorded in the Mishnah (Eduyos 7:7), Rabban Gamaliel the Elder—the son of Hillel's son Rabban Shimon and the Nasi of the Sanhedrin—went to Damascus to complain to the proconsul Vitellius about the bloody incidents and cruelties of Pontius Pilate, the Procurator of Judaea. These acts of aggression against the Jewish people by the officials of Pontius Pilate could have easily ignited popular uprisings throughout the country. As a result of the peacemaking mission of Rabban Gamaliel and his ability to calm down the people of Judaea, Pontius Pilate was removed from office and the rebellion was prevented.

The 'Birth Pangs of Mashiach' and the Ingathering of the Ten Tribes

Shortly after the death of R. Joshua, a new generation of sages under the leadership of R. Akiva, who had been the most prominent student of R. Joshua, abandoned the peaceful traditional teachings of R. Hillel, R. Johanan ben Zakkai, R Eliezer, and R. Joshua. They enthusiastically greeted the military leader of the Revolt, Bar Kokhba, who R. Akiva declared the long-awaited Jewish Messiah. It may be alarming to many that a rabbi as well known and respected as Rabbi Akiva would rule that the Ten Tribes would not return. In his book *The Messianic Idea in Israel*, Professor Klausner suggests a compelling reason as to why Rabbi Akiva may have taken this position: "R. Akiva held his opinion because he had proclaimed Bar-Kochba as Messiah and was expecting the redemption of Israel through him, while the remnants of the Ten Tribes at that time had not yet returned to Palestine and had no intention of doing so. R. Akiva may have discovered the latter fact on his long journeys to Gaul, Africa, Arabia, and particularly Media, to which the Ten Tribes had been exiled according to Scripture (II Kings 17:6): *"Therefore he was forced to oppose the opinion that the Ten Tribes must return in the Messianic age"* (emphasis mine).

The Talmud says of the anticipation of the Messiah: "When you see a generation ever dwindling, hope for him; when you see a generation overwhelmed by many troubles as by a river, await him" (Sanhedrin 98a). It seems the teachings of God's prophets and sages regarding the Messiah and Messianic Time—its guidelines, signs, and conditions—had been overlooked or only cursorily considered. The 'lost' Ten Tribes were not found. In fact, no one was even looking for them. After all, R. Akiva had officially declared that they had disappeared forever and would never return. Yet, as any student of the Bible knows, the first priority of the Messiah will be the reunification of the Twelve Tribes of Israel and their return to the Promised Land. Acknowledgement of the Ten Tribes, their reunification with the rest of the House of Israel, return to the Promised Land for redemption by the Almighty, and the restoration of the Kingdom of David and his throne (Isaiah 11:12; 27:11; Ezekiel 37:21; 39:28; Micah 4:7; 7:12), are all premises emphatically prophesied in the Hebrew Bible, as well as explained in the Talmud and Rabbinical Literature as necessary for the Advent of the Messiah.

According to the Rambam (Maimonides), the most prominent sign of redemption in the Torah is the ingathering of the exiles: "Then the Lord your God will restore your fortunes and have compassion on you and gather you again from all the nations where He scattered you. Even if you have been banished to the most distant land under the heavens, from there the Lord your God will gather you and bring you back. He will bring you to the land that belonged to your ancestors, and you will take possession of it. He will make you more prosperous and numerous than your ancestors" (Deuteronomy 30:3-5). The return of the exiles is, then, the most important task of the Messiah! As soon as it takes place, the Messiah will undertake the victorious Messianic Wars. Concerning the building of the Temple, there is a dispute among the rabbis and theologians as to which comes first, the Messiah or the Temple. Some scholars say that the building of the Holy Temple will precede the arrival of the Messiah. In his Letter to Yemen, Maimonides cites the prophecy of Malachi— "For suddenly the master whom you are seeking will come to his sanctuary" (3:1)—indicating that the Messiah will come once the Temple has been built. The sages of the Talmud expressed the same opinion: "The Holy Temple will in the future be re-established before the establishment of the kingdom of David" (Ma'aser Sheni 29). In any event, the purpose of the Messiah's coming—the task of the Redemption and perfection of this World—should be accomplished before his death.

Of the aims and achievements of the Messianic Age, we know the following: firstly, victorious wars will be fought during its early years (Zechariah 9:5-6; 12:6; 14:9-12; Isaiah 11:13-14; 17:1; 34:5, 8; 60:18; Obadiah 1:18; Ezekiel 25:12-17; Jeremiah 48 and 49; Zephaniah 2:8-11); secondly, there will be a reunification with, and ingathering of the Twelve Tribes (Isaiah 11:12; 27:11; Ezekiel 37:21; 39:28) in the re-established Biblical borders of the Land of Israel (Numbers 34:13; Ezekiel 45:1); thirdly, there will be a rebuilding of the Temple and renewal of the sacrificial services (Micah 4:1-2; Isaiah 2:2-3; 56:6-7; 60:7; Malachi 3:4; Zechariah 14:20-21). The rest of the tasks—such as turning all peoples to the one God of Israel (Deuteronomy 7:6-8; 14:2; 30:8, 10; Jeremiah 31:32; Ezekiel 11:19-20; Exodus 19:5-6; Zechariah 8:23), abolishing wars forever, and bringing peace and justice to the world—might be accomplished later (Micah 4:2-4; Hosea 2:20; Isaiah 32:16-18; Jeremiah 33:9; Psalms 86:9). Whoever fulfills these goals, will have been legally qualified by Scripture to be the true Messiah. According to Maimonides, the Messiah does not have to perform signs, wonders or miracles. If any anointed King of Israel performs all of the aforementioned tasks, we shall be able to surely say: this man is the Messiah anointed by God!

The Judeans as a nation were not totally repentant and righteous. Neither were they totally evil and sinful. They were not ready, 'not ripe' for God's Redemption. The prophesied time for the Messianic Age had not come yet. There was no arrival of the Prophet Elijah who is supposed to appear before the Messiah to 'turn the heart of the fathers to the children, and the heart of the children to their fathers' (Malachi 4:5-6). The internal situation in Judaea was not even close to exhibiting the signs described in the Talmud as comprising the birth pangs of the Messiah.

In the Talmud the situation of the 'Birth Pangs of Mashiach' is aptly described this way: "In the Footsteps of *Moshiach* (the Messiah) insolence will increase and honor dwindles. The vine will yield its fruit abundantly but wine will be expensive. The government will turn to heresy and there will be none to offer them reproof, the meeting places will be used for immorality, the Galilee will be destroyed, the Gavlan (cities along the border of Israel) desolated, and the dwellers on the border will wander about from town to town without anyone to take pity on them, the wisdom of the learned will degenerate, fearers of sin will be despised, and the truth will be lacking, youths will put old men to shame, the old will stand up in the presence of the young, a son will revile his father, a daughter will rise up against her mother, a daughter-in-law against her mother-in-law, and a man's enemies will be the members of his household, the face of the generation will be like the face of a dog, a son will not feel ashamed before his father, so upon whom is it for us to rely? Upon our Father who is in Heaven" (Talmud, Sotah 49b).

Furthermore, the oldest Midrash Pirkei de Rabbi Eliezer (Chapter 32) and Yalkut Mechiri (Psalms 177) predicts that the children of Ishmael will initiate chaotic wars against Israel in the future and bring much harder and more devastating disasters upon the Israelites than the previous two. During this time the Messiah from the House of David will be revealed. In connection with prophesied future problems for Israel from the Arab and Muslim countries, Rebbetzin Esther Jungreis wrote: "It is written that, before the coming of Messiah, we will have to contend with a fifth source of tribulation that will come from Yishmael—the Arabs—who will inflict terrible suffering on the world and on our people. This teaching is reaffirmed by Rabbi Chaim Vital, the illustrious disciple of the Arizal, who wrote that before the final curtain falls upon the stage of history, Yishmael will inflict torture on our people in ways the world has never before seen. One need not have great powers of discernment to recognize the painful veracity of these predictions. Consider only the suicide bombers, the decapitations, the hijackings, the missiles, the rockets, and the constant, senseless brutal acts of terror."

R. Akiva mistakenly understood the time of Hadrianic persecutions as the darkest moment of Judaean history. For him this turbulent time, with its succession of troubles, woes and sorrows for the Jewish people under ruthless Roman oppressors showed that the situation had reached 'the bottom of the pit,' the Eve of Redemption and the Messianic Age. *It is important to note here that Hadrian's worst religious persecutions (i.e. evil decrees) had begun the aftermath of the crushed rebellion of Bar Kokhba.*

The time of the 'birth pangs of Mashiach' will affect not only the Jewish people but also all nations of the world. Rabbi Yitzchak said: "In the year that *Melech HaMoshiach* will be revealed, all the kings (leaders) of the nations will be struggling against each other." Our Sages taught: "When *HaMelech HaMoshiach* [the King, the Messiah] will come, he will stand on the roof of the Beis *HaMikdash* [the Temple] and call out to the Jews, 'Humble ones, the time for your redemption has come'" (Yalkut Shimoni Remez Yishayahu 499).

Panic, chaos, confusion, wars and dramatic disasters will become the unbearable reality of the day. All the nations of the world will tremble and shake and fall on their faces. They will be seized by pains like labor pangs. In this outraged state of darkness and chaos the Jewish people will ask, "What to do? Where do we go?" God will answer them, "Why are you afraid? Do not be afraid, for the Time of your Redemption has arrived. Everything that I did, I did only for you. Nor will this redemption be like the first [from Egypt]. For the final redemption will not be followed by any further suffering or servitude to the nations" (ibid.).

The first Exodus from Egypt eventually ended with destruction and Assyrian captivity for the Ten Tribes of Israel. The second Exodus of the Jewish people from Babylon also ended tragically with the loss of Judaea's independence, Greco-Roman domination, the destruction of the Second Temple, and 2,000 years of exile with unparalleled persecutions. Of the third return from exile, which started in 1948 with the creation of the State of Israel as the first stage of the final Redemption, the sages of the Talmud say, "Humble ones, the time of your Redemption has come" (Yalkut Shimoni Remez Yishayahu 499).

The Signs and Times were Wrong

Was the situation in the time of R. Akiva and Bar Kokhba, including the Revolt of 132 to135CE, evocative of the prophesied Messianic Age? Not at all! The Roman Empire ruled the world with an iron fist. Their tempered-in-battlefield, strongly disciplined legions were stationed in the most strategically important parts of the Empire, ready to react to any attempt of the conquered nations to challenge the power of Imperial Rome. The Roman activities of building roads, amphitheaters, stadiums, and temples, together with their minimal non-intervention in the internal affairs of the provinces and tolerant rule of law, won the nations' favor. While there were some wars and military skirmishes in various places, especially with the Parthian Empire, they did not last long and often ended with peace treaties. In the interest of Rome, Emperor Hadrian decided to re-establish his eastern borders up to the Euphrates, and willingly returned the disputed territories of Armenia and Mesopotamia to the Parthian kings. His decision helped to maintain peace with Parthia for at least half of the century.

It is because of the absence of the Messianic signs taught by Scripture, Rabbi Yochanan ben Torta, a *Tanna* of the same generation, was a fierce opponent of Bar Kokhba and his Revolt against the Roman Empire, and argued against R. Akiva's decision to announce the Messiah and the Messianic Era. He famously said: "Akiba, grass shall grow from your jaws and yet the son of David shall not appear" (Jerusalem Talmud, Tractate Ta'anit, 4:8, 68d). To his question of why the First Temple was destroyed, R. Yochanan ben Torta answered, "Because of idolatry, sexual licentiousness, and the spilling of blood within. But this previous Temple (the Second Temple) we knew the people of that era. They were diligent in Torah study, and careful with tithes. Why were they exiled? Because they loved their money and [every] man hated his neighbor" (Tosefta Menachot 13:22).

In the time of the Second Temple the Jewish people were engaged in studying the Torah, keeping the Commandments, and performing good deeds. They followed the letter of the Law but missed the essential spirit of the Law—the spirit of God's love to fellow man. Where God's love is absent, so too is mutual respect, with the result that the evil roots of jealousy, senseless hatred, and sectarian rivalry emerge. As we read in the Yoma, "causeless hatred is considered of equal gravity with the three sins of idolatry, immorality, and bloodshed together" (9s).

The destructive presence of causeless hatred is why the Second Temple was destroyed. The sages teach that every generation in which the Temple is not rebuilt is as wicked as the generation in which it was destroyed; for were we worthy, the Temple would have been rebuilt in our days (Jerusalem Talmud, Yoma 5:1). The rabbis see the destruction of the Second Temple not as a failure of the Jewish people to study the Torah, but to live the Torah. Meanwhile, the situation was no different for the generation of Bar Kokhba Revolt including R. Akiva's disciples. The Messianic signs were almost the same as in the time of the First Great Jewish Revolt of 66 to 70 CE and, as in the past, rebellion against the Roman Empire led to catastrophic defeat and slaughter.

The Talmud Praises Rabbi Akiva and Compares him to Moses

R. Akiva may have known these signs better than anyone else. As the greatest sage of his time, the pillar of the Oral Law, the most influential and famous among his contemporaries, R. Akiva ought to have known the conditions of the coming of the Messiah. R. Akiva is portrayed as a sage who was able to gaze at the innermost divine secrets of the Torah, secrets so powerful that similarly great sages could not enter the *Pardes* (Paradise) and leave unharmed. Because R. Akiva was able to enter and exit the Pardes in peace, he not only acquired a unique knowledge of the divine, but he also developed a profound understanding of the world.

The Talmud elevates the image and personality of R. Akiva to heights of greatness and wisdom that altogether exceed even Moses to whom God had spoken 'face to face'. As the Midrash remarks, "Things that were not revealed to Moshe were revealed to Rabbi Akiva" (Yalkut Shimoni, Yishayahu 452; Numbers Rabbah 19:6). R. Akiva has been portrayed as the "brightest star in our large constellation of Rabbis." R. Tarfon said, "Akiva, of you Scripture says, 'The thing that is hid, bringeth he forth to light'"

[Job 28:11]. Others are similarly effusive in their praise: "Happy are you, Father Abraham, that Akiva came from your loins" (Sifre Beha'alotekha 75). And elsewhere: "Akiva, whoever disengages from you, disengages from life" (Babylonian Talmud, Kiddushim 66b; Tosefta). R. Doza ben Harkinas stated that R. Akiva's fame spread "from one end of the world to the other."

According to the Talmud, God told Moses of the rise of Akiva many generations in the future, and of his interpretation of all kinds of laws. "Master of the Universe, show him to me," asked Moses. God said, "Turn around." Moses went and sat in the eighth row of students in R. Akiva's class, and had no idea what they were saying" (Melachot 29b). There is an opinion that "the Halakhah agrees with Rabbi Akiva even over his teacher" (Babylonian Talmud, Ketubot 84b). This passage implies that even Moses did not understand the Torah he received from God on Mount Sinai as compared to the Torah taught in the Academy of R. Akiva.

Arguably, there is no wise man in the whole history of Israel who could excel Moses in greatness as a prophet or as a teacher of Judaism. This humble man, the humblest who ever walked this earth, the true hero of the Israelites, and unsurpassed spiritual leader of the nation, has a legacy that will endure into eternity. As the Chief Rabbi of Great Britain Lord Jonathan Sacks says, "Then Moses knew he had made a difference. Little could he have known that he—who encountered almost nothing from the Israelites in his lifetime but complaints, challenges and rebellions—would have so decisive an influence that the people of Israel 3,300 years later would still be studying and living by the words he transmitted; that he had helped forge an identity that would prove more tenacious than any other in the history of mankind; that in the full perspective of hindsight he would prove to have been the greatest leader that ever lived." It was Moses with his speaking impediment—he frequently stumbled over the words—whom the God of Israel sent to Pharaoh to bring the Israelites out of Egypt.

As he said to the Lord: "Who am I that I should go? I have never been eloquent, neither before, nor since You have spoken unto your servant: but I am slow of speech and of a slow tongue" (Exodus 3:11; 4:10). Despite not being a good speaker, a 'man of no words,' the words of Moses are engraved forever in the divinely inspired Hebrew Bible.

In his "Thirteen Principles of Faith," Maimonides expressed belief in the truth and greatness of Moses' prophecies. Significantly, the numerical value of 'Moshe Rabbeinu' is 613, the exact numbers of *mitzvoth* (commandments) that Moses received from God. If other prophets communicated with God by means of miraculous visions and nightly dreams, Moses is the only prophet who ever knew God 'face to face', to whom God spoke directly: "Hear now My words: If there is a prophet among you, I, the LORD, make Myself known to him in a vision; I speak to him in a dream. Not so with My servant Moses; He is faithful in all My house. I speak with him face to face" (Numbers 12:6-8). To prevent people from worshipping Moses (which is a form of idolatry), God left his grave unmarked (Deuteronomy 34:6). Moses' prophecy offers an important description of the Messiah's reception among the people: "The Lord your God will raise up to you a Prophet from the middle of you, of your brothers, like to me; to him you shall listen" (Deuteronomy 18:15). A future Messiah will be a prophet like Moses. He will speak on behalf of God, convey His word to people, and act as a mediator between God and men. He will be an Israelite, and his discourse will compel obedience. Do these characteristics of the Messiah-prophet correspond to Bar Kokhba, R. Akiva's chosen Messiah?

In contrast to Moses, R. Akiva's tragic mistake was in acknowledging the wrong man as God's chosen Messiah. His fundamental misjudgment leads one to wonder if he was indeed the "Head of all the Sages," as he has been called. Rabbi Yohanan ben Torta sarcastically said to R. Akiva of his decision to proclaim Bar

Kokhba the Messiah: "Akiva, grass will grow on your cheeks and still the son of David will not have come." This rabbi's confidence was certainly based on the teaching of Scripture concerning the advent of the Messiah and the Messianic Times.

Indeed, it is shockingly surreal to think about the greatest spiritual and scholarly sage of that time—someone of the caliber of R. Akiva—co-organizing a Jewish Revolt that was not sanctioned by the God of Israel. To calculate the Messianic Times and try to force the hand of Divine Providence by promoting a self-made Messiah is clearly forbidden. Great thinkers can make erroneous judgment regarding religious, political, and national issues. There is no infallible person in Judaism. But it is hard to imagine R. Hillel the Great, R. Yochanan ben Zakkai, R. Joshua ben Hananiah, R. Yohanan ben Torta, R. Eliezar of Modiin or R. Judah the Prince—all of them great Rabbis, wise scholars, and spiritual teachers of Israel—becoming involved in self-appointed political Messianism, declaring the wrong Messiah, and engaging in armed struggle against the mighty Roman Empire.

The Revolt of the Maccabees

Some people may raise an objection to this argument by pointing to the Revolt of the Maccabees against the Greeks in 167 BCE. This successful uprising was begun and led by the priest Mattathias and his five sons. The lives of Mattathias and R. Akiva do not initially invite comparison. Mattathias was a priest—as a Cohen from the priestly class—and a descendant of Aaron. He also was the elder of the town Modiin where the Revolt originated. By no means was he a renowned scholar, spiritual leader, or influential teacher of Israel. What he had in common with R. Akiva, however, was an uncompromising love for the God of Israel and His Torah.

There was no power in the world that could have possibly forced them to abandon the religion of their fathers.

Consider the words of Mattathias recorded in the first book of Maccabees: "Even if all the nations that live under the rule of the king obey him, and have chosen to do his commandments, departing each one from the religion of his fathers, yet I and my sons and my brothers will live by the covenant of our fathers . . . We will not obey the king's word by turning aside from our religion to the right hand or to the left." (2:19-22)

The Maccabean Revolt was not only directed against the Greeks, but also their fellows Jews, who had become Hellenized idolaters scornful of Judaism and allies with the Greeks. The significant difference between the Bar Kokhba Revolt (132-135 CE) and the Maccabean Wars (167-142 BCE) is that the God of Israel was not with R. Akiva, his spiritual army of learned students and the freedom fighters of Bar Kokhba in their battles against the Romans. Hence their brutal defeat and exile. Meanwhile, there is much evidence that the Almighty was on the side of the Maccabees in their 25 year-long struggle against the Greek Seleucid Empire of Antiochus IV Epiphanes (c. 215-164 BCE). The Maccabees were successful in regaining the independence of Judea and establishing the Hasmonean Dynasty after 500 years of subjugation. How do we know of their success? We know it by the historical accounts and descriptions found in the first and second Books of the Maccabees.

After Mattathias started the Revolt with the shout, "Follow me, all of you who are for God's law and stand by the covenant" (1 Maccabees 2:27), he with his five sons and those who joined them fled to the wilderness of Judea. They were able to organize an army of 12,000 poorly trained peasants with primitive weapons and no war experience. Their first battle was against a 40,000-strong professional Greek army of well-equipped, trained, and battle-hardened soldiers assisted by a herd of war elephants, 'the tanks' of the ancient world. Despite all these disadvantages, the Maccabees miraculously won the battle. Just compare it with the last battle of the Bar Kokhba army at Bethar, when 80,000 Roman soldiers besieged and defeated 200,000 Jewish rebels. Some even say that it was 400, 000 fighters: 200,000 with dismembered fingers and 200,000 of those who could uproot a cedar tree while riding a horse. (Jerusalem Talmud, Ta'anit iv. 68*d*).

What were Bar Kokhba and his soldiers saying before they were committed to battle? "O Lord God of Host, do not stand at our right hand, nor be against us, for You, O God, have abandoned us. We ourselves shall be victorious over the enemy." These words are tragic and pessimistic. God's spirit was absent from the hearts of these rebels. They had a presentiment that their rebellion would end in catastrophic defeat and massacre. The Maccabees had a different attitude towards the God of Israel. They substituted their shortages in number of fighters, poor equipment and lack of training with love for the God of their fathers and an unbreakable will to fight to the death for the divine cause. They did not rely only on their physical strength, arrogance of power, and belief in themselves; they completely trusted in the God of Israel. That is why the Almighty was with them. That is why they were victorious in their fight against the Greeks.

"Who is like You among the powers O God!"—was the battle cry of the Maccabees. These words belong to the leader of the revolt, Judah the Maccabee, who was called "the Hammer." Their battle cry reveals a huge spiritual difference between them and the participants of the Bar Kokhba Revolt. Even Rabbinical legend differentiates between heroes such as Bar Kokhba or Samson, characterizing them as *'gibborim'* (meaning "mightiest") and the Maccabees Zealots, whom the legend calls royal "kings."

Perhaps *Chanukah* is the clearest manifestation of the military and spiritual miracles that the God of Israel performed in order to help the Maccabees in their highly spiritual fight. A compelling miracle happened in 164 BC, when the Maccabees recaptured Jerusalem and purified the Temple. The Talmud describes this event that gave birth to the miraculous festival of *Chanukah*: "and when the royal Hasmonean House gained the upper hand and vanquished them [the Greeks], [the Hasmoneans] searched and found only one flask of oil with the Kohen Gadol's [High Priest's] seal, and it contained only [enough oil] to burn for one day. A miracle occurred and it burned for eight days" (Talmud, Shabbat 21b). Here is another description of the dedication of the Temple by Judah Maccabee and his brothers, "After having recovered Jerusalem, Judah ordered the Temple to be cleansed, a new altar to be built in place of the polluted one, and new holy vessels to be made. When the fire had been kindled anew upon the altar and the lamps of the candlestick lit, the dedication of the altar was celebrated for eight days amid sacrifices and songs" (1 Macc. iv. 36). The God of Israel performed these miracles to help the Jewish people preserve the religious faith of their fathers and achieve independence from the pagan Greeks. Surely, it was God's war, and without question, He presented Himself alongside His people, the Maccabees.

The Optimism of Rabbi Akiva

There is no doubt that R. Akiva had sincerely thought that it was the Messianic Time, that Bar Kokhba was the Messiah who would be victorious over the Romans and bring the Jewish People to freedom and independence. As a truly devoted patriot and nationalistic Jew, he believed that God's people were spiritually ready for redemption and there was nothing in the world that could stop them from achieving their goals. The realization of his dream required an organized army of brave and determined

Jewish fighters who loved the God of Israel, were enlightened by knowledge of the divine Torah, and were ready to die for the cause.

In his article titled "Rabbi Akiva's Optimism," R. Meir Soloveitchik writes: "Why was R. Akiva so certain that redemption was at hand? Maimonides, the leading Jewish philosopher of the medieval period, looked to the Talmud when he wrote that Israel will be redeemed only if it repents; in other words, redemption will occur only if Israel deserves to be redeemed. This notion that redemption depends on the worthiness of the Jewish people allows us, perhaps, to suggest that R. Akiva's belief that the Messianic Era was at hand reflected his optimism regarding the spiritual state of the Jewish people. Unfortunately, the acrimony that marked internal Jewish relations prior to the Temple's destruction existed, to some extent, according to the Talmud, in R. Akiva's time as well. Indeed, the death of legions of R. Akiva's disciples is attributed, above all, to their own moral failings." Maimonides concluded, on the basis of Scripture, that Israel will be redeemed only if its peoples repent and turn away from sin. Then, and only then, will God send the Messiah. R. Akiva simply misjudged his generation, which, according to the Talmud, was not ready for God's Redemption. The gathering of the twelve Tribes will be a Divine mission of the Messiah (Isaiah 11:12; 27:13; Ezekiel 37:21; 39:27; Zechariah 10:10; Micah 7:12). Should not the Prophet Elijah come before the advent of the Messiah?

Russian Commissars, Politruks, and the 24.000 Students of R. Akiva

Shortly before Judaea exploded in massive armed revolt, R. Akiva seems to have realized that the rebels did not meet requirements of the Torah in their behavior towards each other. There was no spiritual unity, no brotherly love, and no common respect. These problems were especially manifested in the aftermath of the few initial military victories over the Roman legions, including the conquest of Jerusalem, and the establishment of Judaea's independence. Jews thought that the war was over and the taste of victory made them behave arrogantly. Their attitude is described in the Bible, as it written, "By my strength and my valor I did this" (Deut. 8:17). They showed no respect and love to their fellow men. Each leader claimed his own great credits and merits in the rebellion and, of course, all of this ended in sectarian rivalry and baseless hatreds, which, according to the Talmud, led to catastrophic defeat with dramatic consequences.

At this point in the rebellion R. Akiva decided to strengthen the morale of the soldiers and rectify their behavior and attitude by lifting it up to the highest level of spirituality required by the Torah for God's redemption. He knew that the war was far from over and that the Romans would regroup and attack the rebels with more legions and more sophisticated forces. For this reason he sent his learned spiritual army of 24,000 disciples to join the armed forces of Bar Kokhba. The Torah scholars were supposed to cement the fighting spirit of the rebels, enlighten them with knowledge of God and His Torah, and cause them to irrevocably believe in the Messiah, his victories in war, and the coming of a Messianic Age of freedom, justice, and peace.

In Communist Russia there was an institute of '*commissars*' or '*politruks*' who were sent by the Communist Party to the Red Army with the purpose of strengthening discipline, consolidating unity, and reinforcing the fighting spirit of the soldiers. They would fulfill their goals by ideologically 'brainwashing' the soldiers to follow the 'sacred' and 'noble' cause of the Party. On many occasions they were to show personal examples of love, brotherhood, and heroism, and often sacrificed their own lives for a 'bright Communist future of Humanity.' Communism was their purpose in life and their inspiration.

R. Akiva's 24,000 disciples, who were sent to join the army of Bar Kokhba, had a parallel mission. The difference was only that the God of Israel was supposed to be their love, life, and inspiration. They failed miserably in their mission and paid for their sinful behavior with death by the Roman sword. R. Akiva admitted that his "disciples died only because they begrudged one another the knowledge of Torah" (B. Yebamot 62b). The students had become envious of the Torah achievements of their peers and coveted that which belonged to others. Of R. Akiva's disciples, Rabbi Pinchas Stolper opines: "These outstanding scholars would become the real 'army' of the Jewish people, a spiritual and moral force that would bring the Torah to the entire world, overcoming anguish, suffering, and the cruel boot of the corrupt Roman Empire. They would soon inaugurate a new era of peace, righteousness, and justice, an era in which 'the Knowledge of G-d would cover the earth as water covers the seas'" (The Mystery of Lag Ba'Omer).

In *Meshichei Sheker u-Mitnageidheim* (False Messiahs and their Opponents, pp. 676-681) R. Hamberger includes a long list of people who agree with the Rambam that R. Akiva was the 'weapons bearer' for Bar Kokhba the King, who, as is well known, fought against the Romans (Hilkhot Melakhim 11:3). R. Akiva was undoubtedly the chief spiritual ideologue of the Revolt. Y. Derenberg concludes that R. Akiva and his students were very much involved in the Bar Kochba Revolt (*Maseh Eretz Yisroel*, pp. 220-228). Aharon Heyman also says that R. Akiva and his students were actively involved with Bar Kokhba *(Toledot Tanaaim ve-Amoraim* 3, pp. 1002-1004). R. Eliezer Dunner says that R. Akiva was a strong supporter of Bar Kochba. He suggests that R. Akiva's students were soldiers in his army to fight the Romans and they died during the period of the *Sefirah* (*Zichron Yosef Tzvi*).

Many scholars do not think that the cause of the students' death was the ill-fated plague 'askera.' They give an alternative, more straightforward answer: R. Akiva's 24,000 students fell from the Roman sword on the battlefield as freedom fighters of the Bar Kokhba army during the Jewish uprising of 132 to135CE. It was their spiritual leader and master who sent them to fight as soldiers under the Nasi, Bar Kokhba, whom R. Akiva proclaimed to be the King Messiah.

The Kabbalah mystics have interpreted this story differently. According to them, the tragedy of 24,000 students began many centuries ago in the time when Jacob with his entire family returned from *Paddaraman* (Mesopotamia) and pitched his tent before the city of Shechem whose inhabitants were Hivites. Dina, the daughter of Leah and Jacob, went out to see the daughters of the land. When Shechem, the son of Hamor, prince of the country, saw her, he took her and raped her. Two of the sons of Jacob, Simeon and Levi, Dinah's brothers, took vengeance, boldly attacked the city and slew all 24,000 male inhabitants (Genesis 34:1-2, 25).

From this tale the Kabbalists jump to another Biblical story a few centuries ahead, when Israel abode in Shittim and the people began to commit whoredom with the daughters of Moab. Zimri, the son of Salu, a prince of a chief house among the Simeonites, openly, in front of all congregation of the children of Israel and in the sight of Moses, brought a Midianite princess Cozbi in his tent and started making love to her. When Phinehas, the son of Eleazar, the son of Aaron the priest, saw it, he took a javelin and killed both of them. His actions pleased God, and the plague that was killing the children of Israel was stopped. But before this happened, the plague had already consumed 24,000 Israelites of Simeon's tribe (Numbers 25:1, 7-9

How do the Kabbalists connect all these Biblical episodes with the tragic event of the 24,000 R. Akiva' students that took place almost two thousand years later? According to their fundamental, mystical tradition of *Gilgul*, i.e. transmigration or reincarnation of souls, the 24,000 students of R. Akiva are the same group of people or, to say it more correctly, the same souls of the slain inhabitants of the city of Shechem (Dinah's affair) and the Israelites of the tribe of Simeon (Zimri-Phinehas case). The souls of the Shechemites were taken to the heaven, as all souls of the dead people, and claimed in front of heavenly court that they were killed unjustly. God sent them back on earth for test in the time when Israel committed transgression with the daughters of Moab. Their souls were reincarnated in the tribe of Simeon, specifically because Simeon was the organizer and executor of their massacre. The prince Shechem became the chief of the tribe Simeon. All Israel withstood the temptation, but the tribe of Simeon failed. They were killed; their souls were taken back to heaven and begged God to give them the third (last) chance for correctness. That is how they become the 24,000 disciples of R. Akiva. Furthermore, the soul of Shechem-Zimri reincarnated into R. Akiva himself; the soul of Dinah-Cozbi was reincarnated into Rufina, the converted third wife of R. Akiva. In a same manner the Kabbalists declare, for instance, that the souls of Moses and Jethro are the reincarnations of Abel and Cain; David and Bathsheba, of Adam and Eve and so on. "There is no solid proof of the existence of the doctrine of *Gilgul* in Judaism during the Second Temple period," stated Jewish Virtual Library. The greatest medieval sages also rejected this doctrine: Saadiah Gaon, Abraham ibn Daud, Joseph Albo, Abraham ben Hiyya, Judah Halevi, Maimonides, Abraham b. Moses b. Maimon, and others. The conclusion of mystics of the Kabbalah regarding R. Akiva and his 24,000 students is such that they did not die as a punishment because of their inability to respect the fellow man and other imperfections, but, on contrary, they killed as a reward for loving the Torah, for complete eradication of their sins (*tikkun*), and successful fulfillment of their mission on earth. So their souls completed Gilgul, became righteous, and deserved to be with God in heavenly Paradise.

The Talmud on R. Akiva's Involvement in the Revolt

The Talmud and Rabbinical Literature do not reveal much, if anything, regarding the exact role R. Akiva played in the Revolt. Nor do they inform us of when and how his relationship with Simon Bar Kokhba started, or what spurred his decision to proclaim the military commander the Messiah. There are no answers to many important questions concerning the political activities of R. Akiva and his disciples before and during the Jewish Revolt. We have to understand that for decades afterwards many of the rabbis were still living in the Roman world and were subjected to its rules and laws. In order to function and teach the Torah in the synagogues and keep Judaism alive, they would have attempted to hide or minimize the actual role of influential religious leaders. Hence, the Talmud speaks of a mysterious plague called 'askera' as the cause of death of the 24,000 disciples. In fact, however, these students died in the battlefield as a result of their armed struggle against the legions of the Roman Empire as the soldiers of Bar Kokhba's army.

The only established official fact concerning Rabbi Akiva's connection with Bar Kokhba, the rabbis insist, is that this famous teacher and spiritual leader of the nation regarded the brave general and patriot as the promised Jewish Messiah (Jerusalem Talmud, Ta'anit 4:6; 68d). He changed the name of Simon Bar Koziba to Simon 'Bar Kokhba' meaning 'Son of the Star', taking it from the verse in Numbers 24:17, "There shall come a star out of Jacob." This prophecy, indeed, is understood as pointing to a future Messiah. Rabbi Akiva undermined the arguments of the Sages of the Sanhedrin and the Academy in Yavneh. He disregarded the opinions of his closest disciples, and failed to heed signs and messages from God in prematurely proclaiming the brave and successful General Bar Kokhba as the Davidic Messiah. His proclamation was intended to arouse and mobilize the population of Judea in support of a rebellion against Rome. This decision, unwarranted by Scripture, drew the Jewish People directly into the Roman massacre.

Despite his fundamental lack of insight on this matter, R. Akiva was an experienced politician who had travelled abroad extensively. He had visited Rome with the co-presidents of the Sanhedrin—R. Gamaliel, R. Eleazar, and R. Joshua—to plead the case of Palestinian Jews before the Emperor Domitian (81-96 CE) during the so-called 'Journey of the Elders' (95-96 CE). He had witnessed the strength and might of the Roman Empire. He knew that the Jews had no chance to success without the God of Israel on their side. As R. Riskin writes, "Indeed, R. Akiva put his ideas and ideals into practice by spearheading the Bar Kokhba rebellion against Rome (app. 135CE) for the avowed purpose of Israel's liberation of Jerusalem and rebuilding of the Holy Temple."

Perhaps R. Akiva ought to have heeded the words of one of his five principal students, who observed, *"He who announces the Messianic time based on his calculation, forfeits his own share in the future"* (R. Jose, in Derek Ereẓ Rabbah xi, emphasis mine). Rabbi Jonathan ben Eleazar also curses those who predict the advent of the Messiah and estimate the end times, "Blasted be the bones of those who calculate the end" (Babylonian Talmud, Sanhedrin 97b).

Some scholars say that the only fact tied R. Akiva to the Bar Kokhba Revolt, is his announcement that Bar Kokhba is the Messiah sent by God: "When Rabbi Akiva would see Bar Koziba, he would say, "This is the King Messiah!" (Jerusalem Talmud, Ta'anit 4:6; 68d-69a; Lamentations Rabbah 2:4). "This [announcement] is absolutely all there is in evidence of an active participation by Akiva in the revolution," insist the proponents of this idea. This seems to be the official position in Judaism about the historical events of the Bar Kokhba Revolt and R. Akiva's mysterious involvement in it. Of course, we cannot accept this statement or any of the other similar versions of it because bit by bit, slowly but surely, we have found many links and hints which have helped to draw a fuller picture of R. Akiva's personality and his participation in the Bar Kokhba Revolt.

Even R. Akiva's act of declaring Bar Kokhba the Jewish Messiah needs more clarification and elaboration. Was Bar Kokhba anointed with the special oil prepared according to the directions of the Almighty (Exodus 30:22-32) in the manner of the Biblical description? Consider the Scriptural description of the Prophet Samuel's anointing of the first King of Israel, Saul: "Then Samuel took a flask of oil and poured it over Saul's head. He kissed Saul and said, "I am doing this because the Lord has appointed you to be the ruler over Israel, His special possession" (1 Samuel 10:1).

How did R. Akiva determine that Bar Kokhba was the man whom it had pleased God to choose as the Messiah? R. Akiva knew him only as a Jewish patriot and talented military commander who had had a few successful victories over Roman legions immediately before and during the initial stages of uprising and had established an independent kingdom that lasted for two and a half years. (This success had caused many other rabbis to believe in him as the Messiah [Sanhedrin 97 b]). How had R. Akiva figured out that this person, posing as the Messiah, had established such a personal spiritual relationship with God that He had set him apart to accomplish a special divine mission? The Messiah of Scripture is supposed to be a righteous man with highly developed spiritual insight, great virtues and profound understanding of the Word of God. The "spirit of the Lord" will be upon him, and he will have a "fear of God" (Isaiah 11:2). Only a man in possession of these qualities could have been the potential Messiah. They say that Bar Kokhba was not a false Messiah but the one who failed. It would seem that the personality and deeds of Bar Kokhba should have disqualified him from even being considered the potential Messiah.

CHAPTER III

Why is a Full and Factual
Biography of R. Akiva Missing?

Stories and Legends about R. Akiva

Why is a full and factual biography of R. Akiva missing? In lieu of a proper account of his life, the same legends and stories circulate over and over again. These myths recount the same tired tales—of how he met his wife Rachel, whose rich and respected father, Kalba Sabua, employed him as a shepherd of his flock; how the episode of the stone worn away by drops of water changed his life; how his wife was dedicated to his learning and sent him to the Yeshiva of the great Rabbi Eliezer; and how, from having been an illiterate and ignorant person, this poor shepherd (Yebamoth 86b) became the most famous teacher in Judaea, one of the greatest authorities on Jewish tradition and law. We are also told that Rachel and Akiva were so poor that the young wife had to sell her hair to enable Akiva to continue to study the Torah, and that a bundle of straw was only bed they possessed. The legend relates that even this "treasure" they willingly shared with an old man on behalf of his sick wife. This old man happened to be the Prophet Elijah, who had come to test Akiva (Nedarim 50a).

There are many instances when the stories of R. Akiva and Rachel repeat traditional tales as they relate, for example, to R. Eliezer's disinheritance by his father Hyrcanus in the presence of Rabban Yohanan ben Zakkai and Kalba Savua. The betrothal arrangement of their son Yehoshua (Tosefta Ketubot) is uncannily reminiscent of Rachel's dedication to R. Akiva's studies. Rabbi Akiva's daughter had acted like her mother with regard to her husband—Simeon Ben Azzai—obviously allowing him to go away on his studies for a lengthy period (BT Ketubot 62b). During his thirteen years of study in the Academy, R Akiva was separated from his wife with her permission. The terms and length of their separation contrast with the wrongdoings of one of R. Akiva's students, Hanania ben Hakhinai, who had been studying in his Academy for thirteen years without the permission of, or communication with, his wife. The other source says that the wealthy Jerusalemite, Kalba Sabua, was not the father of Rachel. She was the daughter of an entirely unknown man, named Joshua, whose son, R. Johanan, is specifically mentioned as "Rabbi Johanan, son of Joshua, R. Akiva's father-in-law" (Mishnah, Yad Hahazakah 3:5). Rabbi Akiva's son was certainly called Joshua (Tosefta, Ketubot 4:7), probably after his grandfather. The Talmudic sources even insist that R. Akiva was already married prior attending his study in the Academy and had an adult son. Some authors (Shmuel Safrai for example) suggest that the marriage of R. Akiva to the daughter of Kalba Savua is mere literary fabrication.

Unbelievably, at the age of forty R. Akiva had not even known the Hebrew alphabet and had not been able to write his own name. In an article entitled "Rabbi Akiva's Students: What Went Wrong?," R. David Siverberg wonders, "Why would a man of such depth, intelligence and creative genius never step foot into the vibrant study halls until his middle-age years? He never felt even the slightest sense of curiosity as to what Torah wisdom was all about? How can we reconcile Akiva the shepherd's violent fantasies of abusing the rabbis with our gentle, softhearted image of Rabbi Akiva?" Extensive, painstaking research reveals, however, some relatively unknown information concerning R. Akiva that sheds light on mysteries surrounding his life.

The Wish to Bite a Torah Scholar 'Like a Donkey'

Having been inordinately ignorant and uneducated during his first forty years, and having never studied any religious text, as he later confessed to his students, R. Akiva's attitude towards the rabbis was excessively hostile. He used to say: "O that I would find a Torah scholar and bite him like a donkey" or "When I was an *Am ha'Aretz* [an uneducated, ignorant person], I used to say if you give me a *Chacham*, (a Torah scholar), I will bite him like a donkey!" One of his students said, "You should have said 'like a dog' (it is more wont to bite)! "No," objected R. Akiva, "a dog bites but does not break bones—a donkey bites and breaks bones" (Talmud, Tractate Pesachim, 49b). What aims and aspirations could have possibly motivated the forty-year-old illiterate and ignorant shepherd, who had been constantly abused, rejected, and humiliated by his fellow students and teachers? His animosity towards the learned men of Torah almost certainly involved feelings of revengefulness, hatred and jealousy.

For a long period of time—well over a decade—he was ignored at the Academy by the students and leading rabbis. R. Akiva's teacher, R. Eliezer, is known to have been a "very severe and somewhat domineering with his pupils and colleagues, a characteristic which led occasionally to unpleasant encounters" (Sifra, Shemini 1:33; Erubin 68a; Hagigah 3b; Megillah 25b). Who knows how many such encounters R. Akiva had during the early years of his studies? It seems that R. Eliezer, as a conservative upholder of tradition, was supportive of R. Shammai's opinion that "One should teach only someone who is smart, unassuming, of good lineage, and wealthy."

As soon as he become the head of the Academy at Bnei Brak and achieved influence and prominence among the rabbinical religious aristocracy and scholarly social hierarchy, R. Akiva consistently disputed his teachers—including his masters R. Eliezer and R. Joshua—with innovative methods of interpretation on matters of Jewish Tradition and Law. R. Akiva had countless disputes with his teachers and colleagues. A rule was later established: Whenever Rabbi Akiva disputes a single sage the *Halakhic* ruling follows him, but not so when he disputes more than one sage.

There are many stories in the Talmud of the numerous disputes between R. Akiva and the sages of the older generation, many of which involved his conservative teacher and mentor, R. Eliezer. The resentment towards the Torah scholars and the desire to revenge the abuses and humiliations of his earlier years motivated R. Akiva all his life. He was a descendant of General Sisera, a Biblical enemy of the Israelites, whose militarism R. Akiva inherited, as manifested in his ardent support of the Bar Kokhba Revolt and armed conflict against the Roman Empire. He sent his spiritual army of 24,000 Torah scholars to fight the Romans to the death for the freedom and independence of Judaea. As Maimonides wrote, R Akiva was a 'vessel carrier' for Bar Kokhba, disseminating Messianic ideas among the nations and serving as the official ideologue of the Rebellion. *By proclaiming Bar Kokhba as the Jewish Messiah, R. Akiva legitimized the uprising and designated himself its spiritual leader.*

A Dog Can Become a Lion

As the *Midrash* attests, "In this world, one who is a dog can become a lion, and one who is a lion can become a dog" (Ruth Rabbah 3:2). It is true that personal transformation is possible in this world. But it is also true that the luggage of personal character—one's ethics, morals, and the most secretive parts of his inner traits—travel with a person as he or she changes in status or position. As Talmudic wisdom says, "If a peasant becomes king, he will not take his basket off his shoulders" (Megillah 7b).

Certainly R. Akiva brought his own luggage of personal values—the so-called 'basket of a peasant King'—with him as he grew to become the great spiritual leader of the Jewish nation and the most influential teacher of Israel. According to the customary perception of the Pharisees, one would imagine him as a typically proud and arrogant rabbi, looking down with contempt upon the common people. The rabbinical sources, however, say only that R. Akiva left the impression of being a good, kind, and humble man.

However, the *Jewish Encyclopedia* indicates otherwise. It is says that R. Eliezer, R. Tarfon, and R. Akiva lived and taught at city of Lydda (Sanhedrin 32b; Baba Metzia 49b; Rosh Hashanah i. 6). Responsa from Lydda are often mentioned in the Talmudic sources (Tosefta, Mikwa'oth vii, viii end). Despite the reputation that the teachers at the academy enjoyed, *"there seems to have been certain feelings of animosity towards them in consequence of their arrogance, and it was therefore denied that they possessed any deep knowledge of the Law"* (comp. Pesachim 62b; Yer. Pesachim 32a; Yer. Sanhedrin 18c, d; Bacher, "Ag. Pal. Amor." i. 60, iii. 16, emphasis mine). The Talmudic stories about R. Yohanan ben Zakkai and the trial of R. Eliezar demonstrate the negative role that R. Akiva played in those events, the influence of his past, and the dark and secretive traits of his distinguished character and their effects on the tragic fate of his 24,000 disciples.

In the process of becoming prominent among the elite of Torah scholars, R. Akiva bullishly confronted several famous rabbis, resulting in many reprimands from the rabbinical authorities. One of the earliest stories of R. Akiva's humiliation by the earlier generation of sages takes place in the town of Jericho, when Rabban Gamaliel, the head of the Sanhedrin, hosted a gathering of the scholars. The guests were served dates, and Rabban Gamaliel honored the then young scholar Rabbi Akiva by reciting the *brachah achronah*, the blessing after eating. Meanwhile, Rabban Gamaliel and the other sages disagreed about which blessing should be said after eating dates. After the young scholar said the blessing Rabban Gamaliel exclaimed, "Akiva! When will you stop butting your head into Halachic disagreements?" "Our master," Rabbi Akiva replied calmly, "it is true that you and your colleagues disagree in this matter. But did you not teach us that the law is decided according to the majority opinion?" (Berachot 37a). Even at this early stage of his career R. Akiva was in love with the principle of majority rule. Instead of critically examining the issue at hand to find the right solution, R. Akiva chose the easier way of pleasing the majority and avoiding conflict and disagreement. Rabban Gamaliel was upset that R. Akiva decided issues that were beyond his expertise and knowledge. Hence his didactic tone, "When will you stop butting your head into Halachic disagreements?" It seems that similar incidents had displeased and irritated the President of the Sanhedrin on previous occasions.

Another source of discontent was his ideas concerning the Messiah and the Messianic Age. When R. Akiva decided to go ahead with proclaiming Bar Kokhba as the prophesied Messiah, R. Yochanan ben Torta strongly objected and sarcastically ridiculed him: "Akiva, grass will grow from your cheeks and still the son of David will not come" (Jerusalem Talmud, Taanit chapter 4:5 page 68d). One of R. Akiva's five principal students, R. Jose, resolutely declared: "He who announces the Messianic time based on his calculation forfeits his own share in the future" (R. Jose, in *Derek Erez Rabbah xi*). The indictment against predicting the advent of the Messiah and establishing Messianic time was reissued by R. Samuel ben Nahmani, who said in the name of R. Jonathan ben Eleazar: "Blasted be the bones of those who calculate the end" (Babylonian Talmud, Sanhedrin 97b).

There are some scholars who say that R. Akiva was trying to impose his authority and expertise at *Aggadah* by introducing his unusual interpretations and ideas. For such behavior, he was sharply criticized by his colleagues, especially R. Yehuda ben Beteira, who said to him, "You will one day have to give an accounting!" (Babylonian Talmud, Shabbat 96b, 97a). Of the same opinion was Rabbi Ishmael who thought that R. Akiva had some problems in the field of *Aggadah* with his new approach, particularly his exegesis of the words "bred of the mighty" (Psalm 78:25): When these words were recited before Rabbi Ishmael, he said to them: "Go and tell Akiva, Akiva, you have erred!" (Babylonian Talmud, Yoma 75b). This sage did not hesitate to openly censure R. Akiva: "Desist from your statements and move instead to matters concerning plagues and tent impurities" (Midrash on Psalms 104:9). The Talmudic stories reveal that R. Akiva faced solid opposition from the sages on the subject of his professed expertise in Aggadah. Rabbi Elazar ben Azariah said to him, "What are you doing in *Aggadah*? Retract your words and go back to [laws of the impurity of] leprosy and tents"—or, in another translation, "Akiva, why do not you stick to the laws of purity, and live *Aggadah* alone?" (Babylonian Talmud, Chagiga 14a; Midrash Rabba Sh'mot 10:4). By this, he simply meant that R. Akiva was not considered an authority in the realm of *Aggadah* and should return to *Halakhah*. It was for a specific reason that R. Jochanan said, "There is a tradition transmitted by my father not to teach *Aggadah* to a Babylonian or a southerner, as they are uncouth and unlearned" (Jerusalem Talmud, Pesachim 5:3).

One sage, whose sharp criticism and intelligent arguments could not be refuted even by R. Akiva, was Jose the Galilean, his contemporary and colleague. His superiority in disputes was so dominant that he permitted himself to speak with R. Akiva in a such manner, "Though thou expound the category whole day I shall not listen to thee" (Babylonian Talmud, Zevahim 82a;

Niddah 72b; Menahot 89a; Sifra Tsav 33a). R. Tarfon expressed his high esteem of Jose by interpreting Daniel 8: 4-7 as though it contained an allusion to him: "I saw the ram, that is, Akiba, and saw that no beast might stand before him; and I beheld the he-goat, that is, Jose the Galilean, come, and cast him down to the ground" (Tosefta, Miv. 7:11; Sifre, Num. ed. Friedmann, p. 44a). The *Jewish Encyclopedia* records that as a matter of fact, Jose was the only one who opposed Akiva successfully, and the latter frequently abandoned his own interpretation in favor of his opponent's (Hagigah 14a; Pesachim 36b). It is said in the Talmud that Jose was known for his great piety and even performed the miracles for the benefit of the people. If it was drought in Israel, people asked Jose the Galilean to pray for rain, the rain would come straightway. Sick people pray to him for healing (Yer. Berakoth 9b).

The group of R. Akiva's colleagues, including Eleazar ben Azariah and R. Tarfon, was strongly reprimanded by R. Joshua for their criticism of R. Eliezer after the latter's death, "One should not oppose a lion after he is dead" or "You should not seek to confute the lion after he is dead" (Yer. Gittin 83a; Gittin 50a). In other words, why did they refrain from challenging R. Eliezer while he was alive? R. Akiva knew the profound difficulty of the task. The old sage possessed such vast and extensive knowledge of the written and oral Torah that R. Akiva would have been rightfully intimidated by the prospect of confrontation. That is why Yohanan ben Zakkai called R. Eliezer "a cemented cistern which loses no drop of water."

While the sages were suspicious of R. Akiva's views as a whole, they were particularly dubious of his claims that the Ten Tribes of Israel will neither return to the Promised Land nor merit a place in the World-To-Come. R. Eliezer raised an objection that penetrated directly to the heart of the issue: "Like as this day grows dark and then becomes light, so also with the Ten Tribes; now they are in darkness, but in the future there shall be light for them". R. Eliezer's opinion regarding the return of the Ten Tribes was immediately supported by R. Akiva's closest disciples R. Simeon ben Yochai and R. Rabbi Meir. R. Johanan, a well-known third-century Amora, said, "R. Akiva forsook his piety," or "R. Akiva abandoned his love" (Mishnah, Sanhedrin 110b).

Very little known about the years of R. Akiva's childhood and youth. What is known, or more accurately believed, is shrouded in legend and is the subject of many controversies. As one scholar writes regarding the mystery surrounding his life, "Other than the barest of details, we lack any thorough account of his life. What we have, rather, are snapshots, stories about R. Akiva that appear here and there in the rabbinic literature. Pieced together like parts of a puzzle, they allow us a glimpse of his unusual personality, most notably a singular character trait: His extraordinary optimism" (Rabbi Meir Soloveichik). Other sources agree that R. Akiva's biography must remain inadequate and unfinished. The complete biography of R. Akiva ben Joseph, based upon authentic sources, will probably never be written, despite the rich mass of material gathered by rabbinical sources. Only an incomplete portrait can be drawn of the great scholar who marked out a path for rabbinical Judaism for almost two thousand years.

How R. Akiva Married the Wife of a Roman Procurator of Judea

Anyone familiar with R. Akiva is also familiar with the story of Rachel, the woman who would become his wife, and their romantic love story. She was the daughter of Jerusalem's wealthiest man, Kalba Sabua, and played a role in her husband's achievements. Rashi relates the story of how it came to pass that R. Akiva married the wife of Rufus. When R. Akiva grew old, and was almost at the end of his life, he married the wife of the Roman procurator of Judea, Turnus Rufus. How did the marriage come to pass? Well, as the story goes, R. Akiva and Turnus Rufus often debated matters of the Torah, and R. Akiva always bested him. The humiliated procurator, upon his return home, complained to his wife. She decided to defend her husband by tempting R. Akiva which, she hoped, would cause him to stumble. She was indeed a beautiful woman. When she met R. Akiva alone, she tried to seduce him by revealing her naked legs. R. Akiva's respond was very strange: he spat, wept, and laughed. She was shocked: "Why did you act in such a [strange] manner?" R. Akiva agreed to explain the first two actions. "I spat because we both came from a drop of sperm. I wept because death will decay your beauty beneath the earth." It took her a while to get an answer to why R. Akiva laughed. "You see," he explained, "I knew that you would convert to Judaism and I would marry you." So, as it come to pass, after Turnus Rufus died, she became the third wife of R. Akiva and brought him the great wealth of her former husband (Kesuvos 62b-63a).

From the Kabbalistic sources we learn that this woman, Rufina, married R. Akiva while her former husband was still alive. Turnus Rufus took vengeance on R. Akiva and sentenced him to torturous death. Upon realizing that her husband is dead, Rufina committed suicide. Other sources say that she killed herself while R. Akiva was still alive in order not to submit herself to demands of Rufus.

The truthfulness of this Talmudic story is very doubtful. Just as the claim that R. Akiva married the wife of the Procurator Rufus after his death causes the reader to shake his head in perplexity, this story also elicits a response of disbelief. Other accounts tell us that it was the Roman Procurator of Judaea, Rufus, who arrested R. Akiva and sentenced him to a torturous death, which means that R. Akiva died before Rufus. The presumed truthfulness of one story precludes the validity of the other.

Uncertainty and speculation surround other matters of R. Akiva's life as well. Consider the question of the children. Did R. Akiva have children? The Tractate Moed Katan (21b) mentions that his sons died during his lifetime. One of his sons was Rabbi Shimon (Yalkut Shimoni Shmot 18:171). Some scholars suggest that Rabbi Yehoshua was also his son (Shvuot 6a; Seder Hadorot) but other Talmudic sources prove this wrong (Tosfot; Shabbat 150a).

The Talmudic sources also say that R. Akiva had a daughter. Her name is unknown, as it is unrecorded in the primary source material. Her story is documented in the Talmud. Part of this story tells of how she went to the market and overheard one of the fortune-tellers predicting her future: "She is going to die on the very day of her wedding. Mark my word!" As time passed, she forgot the prediction. Before the day of her wedding, tired of various preparations, she entered her bedroom for the night. As usual, she took a golden broach or hair-pin from her hair and stuck it into the wall. Upon waking the morning of her wedding day, she pulled the pin out of the wall and discovered a dead and deadly poisonous snake, which she had accidently killed by penetrating the snake's eye with her golden broach. When she told her father what had happened, R. Akiva exclaimed, "This is indeed a miracle from God!" Then he asked, "Tell me, daughter, what did you do yesterday?" She could not recall any significant deeds, except one: "A poor man came to our door in the evening and there was none to attend to him. So I took my portion of the wedding-feast and gave it to him." R. Akiva was pleased and proud of his daughter's action, exclaiming "You have done a good deed." Thereupon R. Akiva went out and lectured: "But charity delivereth from death: and not [merely] from an unnatural death, but from death itself" (Babylonian Talmud: Tractate Shabbath 156b).

Celebrated as the 'Head of all the Sages' in the Talmud, R. Akiva is considered one of the earliest founders of Rabbinical Judaism and his name is the seventh most frequently mentioned sage in the Mishnah. The son of Joseph, he came from a family of converts and belonged to the genealogical lineage as General Sisera, captain of the army of Hazor (Gittin 57b; Sanhedrin 96b), the well-known personage Haman, and even Amalek (Rav Nissim Gaon commentary to Berakhot 27b). But shrouded in speculation are the exact years of R. Akiva's birth and death. One source gives the years of his life as c. 50 to135CE, and another as c. 40 to137CE. Many scholars think that R. Akiva lived for 120 years in the manner of Moses, Hillel the Elder, and Yochanan Ben Zakkai. Such assumptions—which are Midrashic material, not historical reality—equate him with these famous giants of the Bible and Judaism (Menachot 29b; Yalkut Shimoni; Sifrei # 357). We know from history that R. Akiva was killed during the reign of the Roman Emperor Hadrian (118-138CE). If he was born between 40 and 50CE, one can readily conclude that he lived into his eighties. In order to arrive at the age of 120, one needs to believe that he was born in15CE and died in135CE.

R. Akiva's Arrest and Execution

Legends concerning the actual date and manner of R. Akiva's death are numerous and unreliable. Some authors (Howell Toy and Louis Ginsburg, *Jewish Encyclopedia*) even advise us to disregard them as being without historical foundation. It is said that he died in Caesarea in 135 or 136 CE, subjected to Roman torture where his skin was flayed with iron combs. As he was being tortured, he reportedly recited the Shema prayer. From other sources we learn that he died in 132CE after several years of imprisonment (Sanhedrin 12a).

The year 135CE is most likely the actual date of his death. Talmudic tradition says that R. Judah the Prince was born in the same year and even on the same day that R. Akiva died a martyr's death. It is suggested that the concurrence was a result of Divine Providence: God had granted the Jewish people another leader of great stature to succeed R. Akiva (Mishna, Chagiga 2:2). Rebbi or *Rabbeinu HaKadosh* (our Master, the Holy One) was the only *Tanna* (early Torah sage) known as 'Our Holy Teacher' due to his deep piety. Another circumstance confirming the death of R. Akiva in the year 135CE or even later is the revocation of his proclamation of Bar Kokhba as the Jewish Messiah. R. Akiva revoked his earlier claim after an incident in Bethar when Bar Kokhba killed the righteous R. Eleazar from Modiin, an event immediately followed by the Roman attack and murder of Bar Kokhba himself. These events transpired in the summer (9 of Av) 135CE.

The reason for R. Akiva's arrest by the Roman authorities is yet another unspecified detail. Some say that he was arrested for disregarding Roman laws forbidding the teaching of the Torah; others say that he was charged as the spiritual leader and ardent supporter of the Bar Kokhba Revolt. Still others opine that following the failure of Bar Kokhba's revolt, the Romans prohibited the public study of the Torah, the functioning of the Sanhedrin and subsidiary religious courts, circumcision, observance of Sabbath, the celebrating of Jewish holidays, and gathering in synagogues and other ritual practices. Rabbi Akiva defied these orders and was imprisoned. The Roman officer Tornos Rufus sentenced him to death. What is important to note here is the suggestion that *the Romans initiated religious persecutions against the Jews in the aftermath of the crushed rebellion.* The *Encyclopedia Judaica* is of the same opinion: *"In the years following the revolt,* Hadrian discriminated against all Judeo-Christian sects, but the worst persecution was directed against religious Jews.

He made anti-religious decrees forbidding Torah study, Sabbath observance, circumcision, Jewish courts, meeting in synagogues and other ritual practices. Many Jews assimilated and many sages and prominent men were martyred including Rabbi Akiva and the rest of the *Asara Harugei Malchut* (ten martyrs). This age of persecution lasted throughout the remainder of Hadrian's reign, until138CE" (emphasis mine).

Finally, some believe that R. Akiva was arrested and executed by the Romans in the aftermath of the failed Bar Kokhba Revolt. After brutally crushing the revolt in 135 CE and devastating the Jewish people, Hadrian attempted to root out Judaism, which he saw as the cause of continuous rebellions. He prohibited teaching the Torah law, Sabbath observance, gathering in the synagogues, religious courts, the Jewish calendar, and he executed Judaic scholars. The sacred scroll was ceremoniously burned on the Temple Mount. In effect, he decided to 'solve the Jewish problem' once and for all. In addition, Hadrian abolished circumcision, which was considered a barbaric form of bodily mutilation by the Romans and Greeks. The timing of this Imperial decree may have been well before the Revolt as some authors argue but it is very unlikely.

If R. Akiva was apprehended and kept in prison for several years and executed before the Revolt, then the reason given for his arrest may have been arousing, exciting, and organizing the Revolt as its spiritual leader. We know that the Romans issued religious prohibition laws after the Revolt. Even if R. Akiva was arrested during the Revolt and executed at its end in 135 or 136CE, he still could not have been charged with defiance of the Roman Laws prohibiting the teaching of the Torah because the time of their issue was after the Revolt. Although the official Judaism's guideline of historical events of this period would lead us to believe that R. Akiva was arrested and executed on religious grounds, there is good reason to believe that the real charges against him by the Roman Authorities were mainly political ones as he was an ardent supporter of, and participant in, the Bar Kokhba Revolt. His declaration of Bar Kokhba as the Messiah, King of Israel, would have been enough for the Romans to arrest him for a capital crime and sentence him to torturous death. By acknowledging Bar Kokhba as God's Messiah, R. Akiva had raised the flag of rebellion against Rome. After that, nothing could have prevented approaching disaster for the Jewish people. This declarative act alone served not only as a religious manifesto concerning the fulfillment of Messianic prophecies but primarily as a political rebellion against the Roman Empire and Emperor Hadrian in particular. It was an act of open defiance and a military challenge to the Emperor and the Imperial power of Rome. The Roman Government in Judaea had sufficient intelligence sources to learn about the popular Messianic Movement of the Jews, the announcement of R. Akiva that Bar Kokhba was God's appointed Messiah, and the effects of the revelation on the Jewish people and surrounding nations. Although the exact day of the proclamation is unknown, it most likely happened a few years before the Revolt. The Roman authorities could hardly have tolerated this situation because it threatened their political system. They may have tried to capture R. Akiva and Bar Kokhba and execute them.

The Talmud on the Role of R. Akiva in the Revolt: Religious Duties versus Political Activities

It is important to remember that most of the information about R. Akiva, Bar Kokhba, and their contemporaries, as well as the events of the Jewish Revolt of 132 to135CE have come to us from Talmudic and Medrashic sources. These date from generations after the events. There is a trend in Rabbinical Literature to change some of the facts of R. Akiva's involvement in the Bar Kokhba

Revolt to the extent of saying that he had no part in it whatsoever (the author Peter Schafer, for example). Concerning his extensive travels abroad, the proponents of this idea point out that these travels were not politically motivated to enlist aid, collect money and weapons, or agitate and incite the Jews of the Diaspora for the upcoming Rebellion, but rather R. Akiva travelled outside Palestine for purely religious purposes, particularly to establish the times of the New Moon and the Leap year. His journey, they claim, was needed in order to extend the authority of the *Nasi* (the Palestinian Patriarch) over the whole of the Diaspora and ensure the correct observance of religious holidays at the same time. They say that the traditional passages concerning R. Akiva's proclamation of Bar Kokhba as the Jewish Messiah do not constitute historical evidence, and thereby remove his name entirely from any connection to Bar Kokhba.

R. Akiva's political activities against the Romans, both inside of Palestine as well as abroad, did not escape Roman attention. There were more than enough spies planted by the brutal Governor of Judaea, Tineius Rufus, among the Jews and the other inhabitants of Judaea. A story recorded in the Babylonian Talmud (Shabbat 33a) illustrates the extent of Roman surveillance. The story relates a meeting and discussion concerning the Roman Authorities among R. Akiva's three disciples, R. Judah, R. Jose, and R. Simeon. Unbeknown to them, their private conversation became known to Romans, as it had been overheard by a certain young man, Judah ben Gerim. At one time a disciple of Rabbi Shimon, Judah ben Gerim later turned spy for the Romans. This treacherous man reported the sages' conversation to the Roman authorities. At once they decreed honor and rank for Rabbi Yehudah for speaking favorably of them, exile for Rabbi Jose for failing to do so, and death for Rabbi Shimon, who had dared to challenge them. There were many planted spies, such as Judah ben Gerim, among the Judeans.

The Secret Intelligence Service of the Roman Government in Judaea was to haunt R. Akiva and his closest circle of disciples and seek to bring them to Roman justice, which would have most certainly meant a cruel execution. R. Akiva could not openly carry out his everyday politico-Messianic activities as the avid supporter of Bar Kokhba the Messiah, and the spiritual leader of the Revolt. The Romans would not have wasted much time in arresting and executing all the leadership of the Revolt, if they could have found them. The entire organizational structure of the Revolt, and its military and spiritual leaders, went underground and conducted their revolutionary business through the numerous secret networks of its trusted and faithful members.

Rabbi Akiva and His Students as Political Fugitives.

Was R. Akiva on the run from the Romans, who wanted to arrest and execute him as the main instigator and spiritual leader of the Revolt? Rabbi Avraham Yitzchak HaLevi Kilav thinks so. He analyses the Talmudic story of Berakoth (60b) about R. Akiva's travels and comes to the conclusion that this narrative confirms that R. Akiva was hiding from the Romans who were searching for him all over the Palestine. As the story goes, R. Akiva was traveling on the road. He stopped at a town and tried to obtain lodging at an inn but there was no room available. He went from house to house asking residents of the town for accommodation for the night but nobody would let him in. So what did he do? He went into the neighboring woods and slept there. The next morning R. Akiva discovered that a band of robbers had attacked the town during the night, mercilessly killing people and stealing their money. For R. Avraham Yitzchak HaLevi Kilav it is quite peculiar that R. Akiva, the greatest Torah scholar, the Father of all Sages, goes from house to house looking for a place to sleep and all the people refuse to let him in. What does it mean? It can mean only one thing: that R. Akiva was running from the Roman Authorities. The fact that people refused to provide him with accommodation means that the Romans had imposed the death sentence on anyone who would help or hide R. Akiva. And they who had mercilessly killed the people of the town were not robbers but the henchmen of the Roman Empire. "It is entirely possible that these were Roman soldiers who were carrying out searches for Rabbi Akiva and that a family caught giving him cover could be sentenced to death," says R. Avraham Yitzchak HaLevi Kilav.

We are hardly alone in representing such facts concerning the Bar Kokhba Revolt and its leadership. There are numerous other sources confirming this position. Rambam writes that R. Akiva was the weapons bearer of Bar Kochba the King, who, as is well known, fought against the Romans (*Hilkhot Melakhim* 11:3). It is also reported that R. Akiva traveled the world in order to recruit Jewish youths and collect money in order to help Bar Kokhba. The Talmud (Berakoth) indicates that he was on the run from the Romans. Indeed, most of R. Akiva's students were wanted by the authorities. R. Meir, his leading disciple, fled from the Romans (Iruvin 13) and died in exile (JT Kilayim 9:4). R. Eliezer ben Shammua was one of the known 'Ten Martyrs' executed by the throne. R. Shimon bar Yochai was pursued by the Romans, and R. Yose was exiled. R. Yehuda was the only one who managed to remain on good terms with the authorities. As a result, R. Yehuda was able to teach the Torah to the people of his generation "more so than any of his colleagues," writes Rabbi Avraham Yitzchak HaLevi Kilav in his work *R. Yehuda the Head Speaker*.

According to R. Kilav, the following facts remain in spite of the various mysteries surrounding his life: R. Akiva was indeed the ardent supporter of Bar Kokhba whom he proclaimed as the Messiah; R. Akiva sent 24,000 disciples to help Bar Kokhba fight against the Romans; he travelled abroad to recruit Jewish (and Israelite) freedom fighters and collect money; his five closest students followed in the footsteps of their master in the political struggle against Rome; and all of them (with the exception of R. Yehudah) were actively hunted and persecuted by the Roman Government.

R. Yehuda (Judah) ben Ilai was the only one of the five who did not support the military uprising against the Romans and was not politically or religiously involved in its promoting. The Romans appreciated his attitude and allowed him teach the Torah. He became the most important *Tanna* (Promulgator of the Mishnah) of his generation, and his name is the most frequently mentioned (more than 600 times) in the Mishnah. As a matter of fact, at the beginning of Hadrian's persecutions R. Judah had been forced to escape from his town of Usha and hide himself until Hadrian's edicts were abrogated. It would seem that he learned a lesson and later on was gradually able to win the confidence of the Romans by "his praise of their civilizing tendencies as shown in their construction of bridges, highways, and market-places" (Babylonian Talmud, Shabbat 33a). According to the Talmud, when a dispute arose between R. Shimon Bar Yochai and R. Judah, the decision of R. Judah prevailed. R. Judah valued nothing more dearly than learning the Torah.

Another prominent disciple of R. Akiva was Rabbi Shimon bar Yochai (100-160 CE), also known by the acronym Rashbi. He was the author of the Kabbalistic work, the *Zohar*. His name is the fourth most mentioned in the Mishnah, and like his renowned master he was also involved in political activities against the Roman Government. The Romans placed a price on the heads of Rabbi Shimon and his son R. Elazar. To avoid arrest and persecution by the Romans, Rabbi Shimon was forced, together with his son, to live in a cave in hiding for thirteen years. He had fought the Romans as much as he could and truly followed in the footsteps of his teacher. Both of them had actively participated in politics and in the Bar Kokhba Revolt. Rabbi Shimon continued to defy the Roman rulers even after Bar Kokhba's defeat. He was forced to flee for his life and to spend years in solitary hiding. To paraphrase the words of R. Eleazar the Great (Sukkah 28a), R. Shimon could have proudly said, "I do what I learned from my great teacher R. Akiva." Despite R. Akiva's mistake in designating Bar Kokhba as the Jewish Messiah and taking an active part in the political Messianic struggle against the Roman Empire, which led to catastrophic defeat and slaughter of Jewish people, the highest tribute to this most beloved sage in Jewish history is the fact that the Talmud (Menachos 29a) favorably compares him to Moses.

CHAPTER IV

The Travels of Rabbi Akiva

Why R. Akiva Traveled Abroad so Extensively

"The numerous journeys which, according to rabbinical sources, R. Akiva is said to have made, cannot have been in any way connected with politics. In 95-96 CE R. Akiva traveled to Rome, and some time before 110 CE he was in Nehardea (Yebamoth xvi. 7), which journeys cannot be made to coincide with revolutionary plans." -Wikipedia

This passage is what passes for scholarship on the subject of R. Akiva. With enviable persistence, not only online sources such as Wikipedia, but also multiple Jewish publishers and authors have managed to convey a false and one-sided image of the man. These popular representations completely exonerate and justify his actions in the rebellion, convincing readers that his proclamation of Bar Kokhba as the Jewish Messiah is the only proven fact of his involvement in the Revolt. Clearly, however, this is not the case.

R. Akiva traveled extensively around the Roman world and beyond to persuade Jewish and Israelite communities of his belief in military Revolt against the Romans for the liberation and independence of Judaea, and for the coming of the long-awaited Messiah and the Messianic Age. The purpose of his travels also included recruiting freedom fighters among Jewish and Israelite communities, and collecting money, weapons and supplies for revolutionary needs. Unlike several other sources, the *Jewish Encyclopedia* confirms the depth of R. Akiva's involvement:

"It is thought that the travels of the celebrated teacher of the Law, Rabbi Akiva, were made with the intention of interesting the Jews of the most remote countries in the coming struggle; and these travels extended through Parthia, Asia Minor, Cappadocia, and Phrygia, and perhaps even to Europe and Africa. Preparations devised on so large a scale could hardly have been instituted without organization, and it may therefore be assumed that the leader, Bar Kokhba, was already quietly preparing for this war in the first years of the reign of Hadrian" ("Bar Kokhba and the Bar Kokhba War")

What is of interest in this passage is the suggestion that "preparations devised on so large a scale could hardly have been instituted without organization." Indeed, to recruit and organize an army of freedom fighters, appoint regional commanders, conduct training and impose discipline, prepare caves and hideouts with underground passages, accumulate weapons and military supplies, create an emergency stock of foods, keep regular communications inside Judaea and abroad, and collect money and propagate ideas of the coming of the Messiah and the Messianic Age—all of these activities would have been impossible without careful planning and organization on the part of determined and dedicated people. Bar Kokhba alone, with all his popularity and growing fame, could not have coped with such a grandiose task. To fight against the Romans in the pursuit of freedom and independence, he needed the help of many brave and ideologically reliable comrades-in-arms and like-minded people united by the same ideas. And he found one such person in a great authority of the Jewish law and tradition, the 'Head of all the Sages,' R. Akiva, who—along with the numerous spiritually-inspired legions of his disciples—was a sincere patriot and strongly nationalistic Jew.

As we have seen, the 24,000 students of R. Akiva did not perish as a result of a mysterious plague named '*askera*.' As the spiritual freedom fighters of Bar Kokhba's army they were killed by the Roman's sword in the course of the bloody battles of the Jewish Revolt for Judaean independence. That is why Jewish people mourn for thirty-two days from the first day of Passover to the thirty-third day of Omer, which is the holiday of Lag Ba'Omer, in memory of the heroism of R. Akiva's 24,000 disciples.

We have also learned that R. Akiva was an experienced politician who traveled extensively. During his trip to Rome to defend the case of the Palestinian Jews before Emperor Domitian (Journey of the Elders, 95-96CE) he learned much about politics from meetings with Roman Senators, Jewish authorities in Rome, and many other influential people of various backgrounds and political platforms. Before the revolt he went to Arabia, North Africa, Egypt, Libya, Cyrenaica, Mesopotamia, Cyprus—in short, to many Jewish and Israelite (Ten Tribes) communities—to propagate his ideas regarding the arrival of a Messianic Age, the necessity of rebuilding the Third Temple, and the divine mission of Bar Kokhba as the Redeemer sent by God to bring freedom and independence to Judea by military victory over the ruthless Roman Empire. R. Akiva presented the ideological views of the Bar Kokhba rebellion to Jewish and Israelite communities and to the public at large and gave to the revolutionary movement a sense of spiritual approval and legitimacy.

"The Ten Tribes Will Never Return"

Upon urging the Jewish and Israelite communities and their leaders to join the Bar Kokhba Revolt, R. Akiva was stunned by their indifference and refusal. His feelings of outrage and anger were particularly directed toward the Parthian Israelites, who had a strong army and immense resources that he hoped would be a decisive factor in the fight against the Roman Empire. He knew that without the help of the Jewish communities in the Diaspora and their kinsmen in Parthia, the Judean Revolt would not have much chance of success. With his hopes and aspirations for a free and independent Judaea and a magnificent Third Temple in Jerusalem on the verge of collapse, R. Akiva cursed the Ten Tribes of Israel: "They will never return and they will not merit life in the World-To-Come." As the renowned Talmudic scholar, Professor Joseph Klausner claims in *The Messianic Idea in Israel*: "Rabbi Akiva, as great a sage as he was, was forced into his position on the Tribes by the failure of Bar-Kokhba as Messiah coupled with his knowledge that *the descendants of the Ten Tribes were unwilling to return to Palestine in his day*" (emphasis mine).

It was common knowledge that some of the Rabbis did not lend their support to Bar Kokhba. What is more, they strongly condemned military confrontation with the mighty Roman Empire. They reminded their colleagues of the tragic outcomes of the two previous Roman-Jewish wars and predicted catastrophic results for the Revolt that was underway. They insisted that the signs and conditions for the revealing of the Messiah were not in evidence. The timing was premature and the world was not ready. That generation was not 'ripe' for Redemption. But R. Akiva, together with a new generation of colleagues, the Sages of the Sanhedrin, and the Academy of Yavneh, persuaded multitudes of his followers to accept his ideas of politico-Messianic involvement and the military confrontation with Rome. He won over a majority to his point of view. From then, the preparations for the imminent Revolt steamed ahead at full capacity.

How the Exiled Israelites Became the Parthians

Of the many countries that R. Akiva visited, Parthia was first on his list. This arrangement was not an accident. What is so special about Parthia that caught his attention? To answer this question, it is important to fill in the historical context. After the death of King Solomon in circa 931BCE, the United Kingdom of Israel was divided into two politically independent states: the Kingdom of Israel in the North with the capital city of Samaria, consisting of the Ten Tribes; and the Kingdom of Judaea in the South with the capital city of Jerusalem, consisting of the Tribes of Judah, Benjamin, and most of Levi, commonly known to the world as the home of the modern-day Jewish people. This division took place circa 930BCE (1 Kings 12:19; 2 Chronicles 10:19). Initiated and designed by God, (1Kings 12:15, 24), such divisions will be repaired in the Messianic Era, when He will reunite, ingather and redeem all the families of Jacob. God had a specific reason for allowing this division that we shall fully understand in the future as the divine wisdom of the Creator's Plan.

The Northern Kingdom of Israel lasted 209 years (930BCE-721BCE) before the Israelites, taken into Assyrian captivity in circa 721BCE, somehow mysteriously disappeared from the face of the earth. They became known as the legendary 'Ten Lost Tribes of Israel.' Since then, world chronological history has been dealing with the nation of Judah, of the former state of Judaea, the people of which were later called Jews. Forced into exile by the Assyrians in the time of King Sennaherib, the Ten Tribes were placed in the Median cities of Halah and Habor near the river of Gozan (2 Kings 17:3-6). The precise geographic locations of these places are unknown. The celebrated Jewish-Roman historian Josephus Flavius, writing during the 80s CE, reflected, *"The Ten Tribes are beyond the Euphrates until this day, and are an immense multitude whose numbers cannot be estimated"* (Antiquities of the Jews, book XI, chapter 5:2, emphasis mine).

Why would R. Akiva visit Parthia? Because he was perfectly aware of the existence of the Ten Tribes of Israel in exile and knew their exact location! But what would the Israelites have to do with the Parthian Empire? According to Steven M. Collins and Yair Davidiy, "the Parthians were Israelites who descended from the Ten Tribes of Israel after their relocation to Asia." Parthia, then, was an Israelite Empire situated in Asia. Imperial Parthia, a hidden and forgotten ancient Superpower in Asia, became one of Rome's greatest enemies. The Parthian Empire (247BCE-224CE) was vast: located east of the Tigris and Euphrates Rivers, it included the territories of Mesopotamia, Seleucia, the northeast region of present-day Iran, the Persian Gulf, and the area south of the Caspian Sea. The Parthians never lost territory to the Romans, nor did they lose any wars waged by Rome. Their relationship with the Romans was not always peaceful or stable. At times the two Empires warred with one another in pursuit of territories of mutual interest.

Bar Kokhba and R. Akiva may have believed that a strained relationship between the Parthians and the Romans still existed. Certainly, they hoped that the Jewish Revolt would find full support among the Parthians. Yet these expectations were not realized. As Flavius's insight reveals, the Israelites were Parthians. Parthia had a large Jewish community. The Jews east of the Euphrates kept in close contact with Jerusalem and faithfully dispatched the Temple taxes. The Euphrates River had long been the recognized border between the Roman and Parthian Empires. That is why R. Akiva went to his brethren in Parthia, sincerely hoping to get what he wanted—that is, military support for the Jewish Revolt from the strong Parthian army, which would promise defeat of the Roman Empire and establish a Messianic Kingdom of peace and justice. Instead, however, R. Akiva received the shock of his life. The

Parthians refused to cooperate. They were indifferent to the cause of the Judeans and were disinterested in their Revolt.

The Ten Tribes are Cursed

R. Akiva's persuasion tactics did not succeed. Although he presented the most powerful arguments to win over their trust and brotherhood, and to incline their leadership to yield to his appeals, he could not convince the Israelites of Parthia to support the war against the Romans. He reminded them of their long, shared history, but to no avail. R. Akiva was a lone voice crying in the desert. The Israelites did not heed him. They did not mind giving money, weapons and necessary supplies, but they categorically refused to send their army or any military units to fight against the Romans.

R. Akiva was incredulous. His kindred people, the sons of their common father Jacob, were utterly ignorant of their national heritage, the God of their fathers and His Laws, and the Hebrew Bible and the prophecies. The fate of the Jews, arriving of the Messiah and Messianic Age did not interest them. They were preoccupied with their own everyday problems and concerns, their own gods and beliefs, their Imperial power and politics, their own skirmishes and wars, and with the unity and well-being of their Empire. And, besides, the Parthians were at peace by then with the Roman Empire who had given them back the disputed territories east of Euphrates; they did not want to break the peace treaty and recommence rivalry and bloody wars with their mighty neighbor.

Having witnessed their refusal to help, and realizing that it could spell disaster, R. Akiva could not forgive. In his outrage and disappointment he cursed them: "The Ten Tribes will not return. Just as a day passes and it will never return so too, they will be exiled never to return." In passing such a severe sentence, he denied the Ten Tribes the right to be present at Judgment Day and merit life in the world-to-come (Leviticus 26:38; Deuteronomy 28:29; Babylonian Talmud, Sanhedrin 110b). The Rabbis of the Talmud rightly refuted him. Rabbah b. Bar Hana said in R. Johanan's name: "[Here] R. Akiba abandoned his love, for it is written, 'Go and proclaim these words toward the north, and say, Return, thou backsliding Israel, saith the Lord; and I will not cause mine anger to fall upon you; for I am merciful, saith the Lord, and I will not keep mine anger forever'" (Sanhedrin 110b).

From ancient times the Ten Tribes had been known as rebellious violators of the Commandments, a stubborn and hard-hearted people: "They and their fathers have transgressed against Me even unto this very day" (Ezekiel 2:3). But there was a time when they had known their God and lived by His divine Laws. It was they who had received the divine revelation of the Torah from the hands of the Almighty at Mount Sinai. They are still His chosen People. The Almighty has never broken the Covenant with them and He wants the children of Israel to repent and return to Him: "All who rage against you will surely be ashamed and disgraced; those who oppose you will be as nothing and perish. You, O Israel, My servant, whom I have chosen. Do not fear, for I am with you; do not be dismayed, *for I am your God*. I will strengthen you and help you" (Isaiah 41:8-11, emphasis mine).

The Israelites have known of this possibility of repentance from the time of their inception as a nation. As we read in the Book of Judges, "Finally, they cried out to the LORD for help, saying, 'We have sinned against You because we have abandoned You as our God and have served the images of Baal'" (10:10). Judah and Israel need one another. They must reunite as one nation again. That is what the Almighty wants, and in time that is precisely what will be achieved! (Jeremiah 3:18; Ezekiel 37:22-28).

CHAPTER V

The Disciples of R. Akiva

Why they died

It seems that the Talmud does not tell the whole story of the Bar Kokhba Revolt. Missing is the role of R. Akiva and his 'spiritual army' of disciples and the nature of their death, among other details of political character. But what the Talmud does tell us is the reason for the 24,000 students' demise, which was the failure on their part to accord honor to one other.

How could 12,000 disciples of R. Akiva, as stated in *Aggadah* (Genesis Rabbah 61.3)—or perhaps 24,000 (Yebamoth 62b) or as many as 48,000 (Nedarim 50a)—perish in the war that, by most measures, they should have won? It is easy to say that the disciples died because of envy and jealousy or because of their failure to 'accord honor to one another.' Yet such reasoning ignores R. Akiva's role as their spiritual leader and mentor in their horrible fate. There were many tragic events in Jewish history that resulted in far more deaths numerically—for example, the Spanish Inquisition, the Khmelnitsky pogroms, and the Nazi Holocaust. None of these disasters are commemorated with even one day of mourning. Meanwhile, the mysterious death of R. Akiva's disciples is commemorated every year with thirty-two days of mourning from the first day of Passover to the beginning of the joyful holiday of Lag Ba'Omer, the thirty-third day of the counting of the Omer. Because these days are deemed a mourning period, practicing Jews refrain from dancing, listening to music, cutting or shaving their hair, and celebrating weddings. As is written in the Shulchan Arukh (493), "The custom is not to marry a woman in between Pesach and Shavuot, until Lag Ba'Omer, as during this period Rabbi Akiva's students died."

What is so exceptionally important about R. Akiva's students and their deaths? After all, they were punished by God and perished in a mysterious plague attributed to their failure to 'accord honor to one another.' Does this violation warrant such a terrible penalty from a just and merciful God? Apparently, it does. Anyone who perceives himself as superior to others, who allows his pride and arrogance to govern his existence and is incapable of honoring his fellow man ultimately rejects the entire Torah. God says of such a person, "He and I cannot dwell in the same world" (Babylonian Talmud, Tractate Sotah 5a; Erchin 15b). One either serves God or one serves oneself—and there is no middle ground. One simply cannot have it both ways!

The students' downfall first began when R. Akiva returned to his hometown. Upon perceiving a poor woman (who happened to be R. Akiva's wife, Rachel) coming through the crowd to see their famous master, the pairs of 12,000 disciples refused to let her come closer. When R. Akiva realized what was happening, he said to them: "Make way for her! For my learning and yours are hers" (Nedarim 50a). This simple episode reveals that these students, in their academic achievements and amassing of knowledge as privileged students of the famous sage, had quickly become proud and arrogant towards the poor and uneducated, and particularly women—so much so that they had forgotten one of the highest principles of Torah: treat people with respect, regardless of status or position, and stand in solidarity with those who are vulnerable.

They were not acting in accordance with the values of the Torah, despite calling themselves its scholars.

Why were the disciples arranged in pairs? Some say that R. Akiva attempted to rectify his students' imperfections through such pairings with the aim of achieving proper Torah behavior. His methods did not help. The situation became worse. Rather than share their accomplishments in Torah studies, the students concentrated on their own individual achievements, each thinking that he knew Torah better than the others. They became jealous, arrogant, and disrespectful towards their fellow students, "treating each other stingily and selfishly" (Bereishit Rabba 61:3).

The modern-day theologian, Rabbi Michael Leo Samuel, contends that, "Of all the explanations that seems to make the most amount of sense, Rabbi Akiba not only offered moral support to Bar Kochba, a man he believed to be the Messiah, he also encouraged his vast number of students to join in the apocalyptic battle against the Evil Empire of his day—Rome, as was first suggested by Rav Hai Gaon back in the 9th century CE." In other words, R. Akiva and his "rabbinic cohorts" assumed an active role in the political-military struggle against Rome and, as R. Samuel further states, the "Romans regarded them much like we view Bin Laden and his fanatical terrorist organization Al Qaeda." R. Samuel also suggests that *"Roman leaders hunted the rabbis, especially Rabbi Akiba, since he was in their eyes the chief instigator of the Revolt* [emphasis mine]." He concludes that the reasons for the failure of the Revolt against the Romans included the inability of R. Akiva's disciples "to treat one another with respect," which in turn served as a catalyst for baseless hatred, mistrust and sectarian rivalry among the freedom fighters and introduce political differences into Bar Kochba's ranks: "Perhaps the above historical tragedy may also serve as a grim reminder that religious leaders within the Jewish community should never have tried to politically or militarily realize their fantasies about the Messiah."

In short, R. Akiva's spiritual army of disciples and followers did not uphold the principles of the Torah. Among these are the instructions to "Judge every man favorably" (Torat Kohanim, Kedoshim 19, 15), and "What is hateful to you, do not do to your fellow. This is the entire Torah, the rest is the commentary" (Shabbat 31a). Most important are the commandments to love, respect, and honor one other. The violation of these principles elicited God's displeasure, and as punishment the disciples were killed by the Roman sword. Ultimately, we can conclude that the tragedy of the R. Akiva's students and the Bar Kokhba Revolt lies in the fact that God of Israel was not with them, and the war they waged against the Romans was not a holy war sanctioned by the Almighty.

The Role of Leadership: 'Bring them near the Torah' versus 'Love your fellow as yourself'

There is an old proverb that 'The fish rots from the head.' It is an apt expression that refers to the failure of leadership. There have been many spiritual leaders of the Jewish nation—both before R. Akiva's generation and after it. So too, there have been many different schools of thought, as well as political and religious movements, all with thousands upon thousands of disciples and adherents. And yet we have never heard of such a terrible fate as that which befell the masses of disciples belonging to R. Akiva. Some scholars suggest that the staggering numbers of casualties are merely haggadic exaggerations.

Rather than quibble with numbers that speak for themselves, however, let us look at other, alternative examples of spiritual leadership as a pathway to illuminating what went wrong under R. Akiva's direction. One of the best examples of spiritual religious leadership can be glimpsed from the precepts of the great scholar,

R. Hillel. A famous Jewish religious leader, Hillel the Eldest (110BCE-10CE) was gentle and patient, loved his fellow man, and pursued peace and tolerance, as his precepts reveal: "That which is hateful to you, do not do to your fellow. This is the whole Torah" (Talmud, Tractate Shabbos 31a), and "Be of the disciples of Aharon, loving peace and pursuing peace, loving your fellow creatures, and bringing them near to the Torah" (Pirkei Avos 1:12). As this passage attests, Hillel encouraged love of God's Torah as the spiritual basis for unconditional love of our fellow creatures.

There is a vast difference between R. Hillel's teachings and those of R. Akiva. The latter adopted the former's precept of "Love your fellow as yourself" and made it the great principle of the Torah. He did not say anything new but merely restated what R. Hillel had already said. What is missing here, however, is R. Hillel's additional exhortation, "Bring them near to the Torah," which means that sincere love for one's fellow man is only possible if one loves the Torah and is spiritually uplifted to its heights of holiness and righteousness. One who understands and loves the Torah feels no limitation to spiritual and physical love neither for his fellows in the House of Israel nor for all humankind. If R. Akiva had followed the teachings of R. Hillel including his instructions to 'Bring them near the Torah,' then he would have empowered his disciples to truly love others with the divine essence of God's love as exemplified in Joseph's treatment of his brothers (Genesis 45:1-15).

Of the same speaks the Alter Rebbe, Rabbi Schneur Zalman of Liadi, founder of Chabad, when he discusses the Torah commandment "Love your fellow as yourself." He taught that the source of every Jew soul is in the One God, and these souls are divided only by virtue of the people's bodies. Those who give priority to their body over their soul, find it impossible to share true love and brotherhood with others; but those who find their joy in the soul alone and elevate it over the body, are perfectly capable to fulfill the greatest principal of the Torah to love every man as yourself because "This is the whole Torah, and the rest is commentary" (Rabbi Hillel the Elder).

While R. Akiva adopted this great principle of the Torah as an important Torah mitzvah [commandment], he ensnared it with physical limitations and other various provisions. This water-downed version of love could not prevent animosity, hatred, jealousy, egoism, anger and other kinds of imperfections from entering the heart and mind, leading to the horrible fate of his multiple disciples of death by the plague (Tanya, chapter 12). In other words, R. Akiva accepted the Torah commandment of "Thou shall love thy neighbor as thyself" (Leviticus 19:18; Sifra, Kedoshim 4) as the greatest principle of Judaism, whereas R. Hillel taught that the execution of this command is equivalent to the performance of the whole Law. The latter principle operated on a purely spiritual level, as embodied in the phrase 'Bring them near to the Torah.' When the Israelites become a righteous and holy nation of Priests, a Light to the Gentiles, they will bring the glory of the Lord to the ends of the world (Exodus 19:6; Isaiah 42:6-7). Through God's love to all people the Israelites will bring humankind to the highest level of spirituality, righteousness, and holiness, allowing all people to inherit the wonderful divine kingdom of the Almighty.

Rabbi Dovid Rosenfeld insightfully identifies the fundamental problems with R. Akiva's approach, and its terrible consequences for his 24,000 students. He explains: "We continued with the historical account of the death of the students of R. Akiva on account of not showing proper respect for one another. To this we asked why of all people were the students of R. Akiva—a great proponent of 'Love your fellow as yourself' (Leviticus 19:18)— to fall short in such an area. Finally, we contrasted R. Akiva's principle of 'Love your fellow' with that of his colleague Ben Zoma: 'All human beings are created in the image of G-d' (based on Genesis 5:1). Whereas R. Akiva's principle begins with love of self—and only then (hopefully) concludes with love of all—Ben Zoma's both begins and ends with love of the entire human race. Focusing first on oneself may engender a form of self-centeredness. A narcissistic love of self may inhibit rather than foster love of others. This narcissism, we may suggest, caused the downfall of R. Akiva's students."

The Chief Rabbi of Great Britain Lord Jonathan Sacks says it this way: "Leadership is not about status, popularity, and glory; the function of the spiritual leader in Judaism is to serve God. It is not a pride valued, but humility in a manner of a real leader Moses. The less there is of self in one who serves God, the more there is of God." If R. Akiva would have followed these principles, 24,000 disciples would have not perished. Furthermore, declaring the wrong man to be God's chosen Messiah and then initiating and leading the Messianic War against the mighty Roman Empire— which, as we know, ended in disaster for the Jewish People— are actions that have nothing to do with servicing God but quite the opposite. The Torah expressly prohibits any individual from predicting the date of the Messiah's arrival or calculating the Messianic Times. Whoever does as much unquestionably contravenes the will of God.

The Torah Students and Their Master as Soldiers of the Sword

The Roman Government was extremely intolerant of political dissent. Punishment for criticizing or challenging the Imperial power was severe. The Jewish-Roman historian Josephus Flavius was targeted by Roman censors for his record of the first Jewish Rebellion, and destruction of the Temple and Jerusalem by Titus. The authors of the Talmud were also under censorial pressure and obliged to follow the same pattern of compromising the historical truth to avoid punishment from the Roman authorities and be allowed to teach the Torah.

Regarding the political motivation of the Bar Kokhba Revolt, scholars have little to say. Rabbi Pinchas Stolper is one of the few thinkers to contend that R. Akiva and his disciples were actively involved in political armed struggle against the Roman Empire and were important participants of Bar Kokhba Revolt. R. Stolper identifies R. Akiva as the key promulgator of the rebellion: "One of the greatest Torah teachers and leaders of all time, Rabbi Akiva added a new, spiritual dimension to the war of liberation. He attempted to merge the soldiers of the sword with the soldiers of the Book—his twenty-four thousand students—each a great Torah scholar and leader. Bar Kokhba trained an army capable of igniting the powder keg of rebellion and Rabbi Akiva lit it with one of the most dramatic proclamations in Jewish history—he proclaimed that Bar Kokhba was the long awaited Messiah." By clearly including R. Akiva and his students among the freedom fighters of the Bar Kokhba army, R. Stolper places the failure of the Bar Kokhba Messiahship squarely on their shoulders. He concludes that in expectation of the Messiah, people have to repent and work hard to learn how to treat each other with love and kindness. If we understand the lesson of R. Akiva's students, then we will learn that the coming of the Messiah depends on us. This lesson to which R. Stolper refers is to 'treat others with respect and honor' (B.T. Yebamot 62b).

One of the many silences surrounding R. Akiva concerns the plague that reputedly caused the death of so many of his students. Not one historian of the period, including the famous Flavius, alluded to a deadly plague in Palestine at this time. However, it is difficult to imagine that this plague exclusively struck R. Akiva's disciples. According to R. Nachman of Breslov (1772-1810 AC), the immediate cause of the students' deaths was the plague referred to as '*askera*,' which Rashi translates as diphtheria, or whooping cough. Some scholars translate 'askera' as sword or sicarus.

Is it possible, then, that Akiva's followers did not die from a mysterious plague after all? R. Hai Gaon (939-1038 AC), a well-known rabbi and theologian who served as Gaon of the Talmudic Academy of Pumbedita (Fallujah, Iraq), believes that R. Akiva's disciples died not from a plague but from the Roman sword. According to this interpretation, R. Akiva and his religious followers were essentially a part of a struggle against the Roman Empire for the political independence of Judaea. Rabbi Prof. David Golinkin refers to "quite a few modern scholars who maintain that 24,000 Jewish soldiers (R. Akiva's students) were killed by the Romans between Pesah and Shavuot, except on Lag Ba'Omer which was a military victory." Among these scholars are R. Nahaman Krochmal, Joseph Derenbourg, R.Yitzhak Nissenbaum, and Professors Shmuel Safrai, Aaron Oppenheimer and Haim Licht. Heinrich Graetz (1817-1891) was amongst the first historians to write a comprehensive history of the Jewish people from a Jewish perspective. Concerning the disciples of R. Akiva, he wrote that the term "the students of Rabbi Akiva" does not literally refer to the students of his Torah, but to those who fought alongside him in the Bar Kokhba rebellion.

R. Kook, analyzing the Jewish heroism in the month of Iyar, mentions three different moral foci: *the overt heroism of R. Akiva's students, who fought fiercely for spiritual and political independence against the Romans in Bar Kokhba's forces;* the hidden heroism of the 12,000 martyrs of Speyer, Worms and Mainz during the First Crusade in 1096CE, *and Rabbi Shimon ben Yochai (Rashbi), R. Akiva's student, who was pursued by the Romans because of his part in the insurrection"* (emphasis mine). Rabbi Eliezer Shenvald arrives at a similar interpretation when he says: "Specifically because of his greatness in Torah, *Rabbi Akiva participated, together with his students, in the war against the Romans,* despite the great dangers and opposition of other sages. He himself took an active part, to the point that he became Bar Kokhba's arms bearer" (emphasis mine).

Apparently the Jews came very close to winning the war. Why did they lose in the end? The sages say they lost because they were too arrogant. Having tasted victory, they adopted the attitude of "by my strength and my valor I did this" (Deut. 8:17). Such arrogance also waylaid Bar Kokhba and his soldiers, leading to their tragic defeat.

A Generation Not Ready for Redemption

R. Akiva's generation was not perfect by any means. There was a considerable breach in the relationship between the masses of the unlearned Jewish community and the academics of the scholarly community. During this time various scandals erupted among the rabbinic aristocracy, including the trial and excommunication of the great Rabbi Eliezer—the former teacher and mentor of R. Akiva (Bava Metzia, 59b)—and the impeachment of Rabban Gamaliel II from his position as Nasi (Berakoth, 27b).

A few contemporaries of R. Akiva—great scholars of the Sanhedrin and Academy—were very critical of the generation of the Bar Kokhba Revolt. It is said that Rabbi Tarfon lamented, "I would be surprised if anyone in this generation can take rebuke. You tell a person to take a stick out of their mouth and they'll tell you to take a board between your eyes." Rabbi Eliezer Ben Azarya confessed, "I'd be surprised if anyone in this generation knows how to criticize" (Arakhin 16b). Do such complaints not explain why the spiritual army of R. Akiva's students came to such a tragic end? These disciples would not bring themselves to love and care for one another. The following story reveals as much:

"Did it not once happen that one of Rabbi Akiva's disciples fell sick, and the Sages did not visit him? So Rabbi Akiva himself entered [his house] to visit him, and because they swept and sprinkled the ground before him, he recovered. 'My master,' said he, 'you have revived me!' Rabbi Akiva went forth and lectured: He who does not visit the sick is like a shedder of blood" (Nedarim 40a). R. Akiva is pictured here as a loving and caring leader for whom the well-being of his students is as important as life itself. Somehow, as we will see, this Torah scholar's attitude completely evaporated when it come to his relationship with R. Eliezer during the period of his master's serious illness.

But R. Akiva's lack of respect for the scholars and sages of his generation (recall his activity at Lydd) revealed itself in his disciples' relationships as well. One story tells of a theological debate between R. Tarfon, a well-known and respected Tanna of the generation, and one of R. Akiva's disciples, Yehudah ben Nehemiah. Upon the conclusion of his rebuttal, during which R. Tarfon remained silent, the disciple's face shined with victorious joy and satisfaction. Thereupon R. Akiva said to him, "Yehudah, your face has brightened with joy because you have refuted the Sage; I wonder whether you will live long." As testified by R. Akiva's closest disciple Judah ben Ila'I shortly after this accident, he was told that Yehudah ben Nehemiah had passed away (Menachot 68b).

Jewish wisdom says that "Jealousy between scholars increases wisdom" (Bava Basra 21a). Such was not the case with the 12,000 pairs of disciples. On the contrary, they were envious of the academic success and achievements of others; their jealousy did not promote wisdom. They gradually lost respect for one another, each one thinking that he had attained more knowledge of the Torah than his colleagues and that his spiritual accomplishments were more complete and higher than those of the others. R. Akiva's disciples had forgotten the words of the great teacher R. Johanan ben Zakkai whom the Talmud called 'The Father of Wisdom and the Father of Coming Generations': "If thou hast learned much of the Torah, do not take credit for it; *for this was the purpose of thy creation*" (Aboth 2:8, emphasis mine). There is a Midrashic saying that if Israel does not study the Torah, God will wipe the world out of existence, but if a person has learned much of the Torah, he should not take credit but instead is obligated to teach others; indeed, teaching others is the purpose of his creation. Rather than teaching others (and thus fulfilling their purpose), R. Akiva's disciples refused to share their knowledge of the Torah and stopped visiting sick comrades. They studied the Torah not with the principal aim of knowing God or establishing a proper spiritual relationship among themselves and with the community, but for other reasons—for example, to enhance their status in the eyes of others and increase their power. In this kind of environment the great principle of the Talmud that "Torah scholars increase peace in the world" (Berakhot 64a) could not possibly find its fulfillment.

R. Yochanan ben Torta argued that the generation of the Bar Kokhba Revolt was no better than the generation that suffered the destruction of the Second Temple. Therefore, he concluded, this generation had not merited the coming of the Messiah and the Redemption. According to R. Yochanan ben Torta, R. Akiva's disciples died because, in addition to failing to honor their peers, they withheld their knowledge of the Torah, and exhibited academic pride, egoism, and arrogance. Given their narcissism, how could R. Akiva's disciples please God and achieve their mission?

It is also on account of the sin of the Jewish rebels that the Romans were able to capture the last stronghold of the Revolt, the city of Bethar, and Bar Kokhba was slain. Rabbi Simeon ben Gamaliel would says, "There were 500 schools in Bethar and the smallest of them had no fewer than 500 children. The children used to say, 'If the enemy comes upon us, we will go out against them with our quills and poke out their eyes. And as a result of the sins of Israel, the Romans wrapped each one in his book, and they burned them. From all of them none remained but me" (Jerusalem Talmud, Ta'an 4:8, 69a). R. Gamaliel applied to himself the verse, "My eyes have caused me grief from all the daughters of my city" (Lamentations 3:51).

What example of holiness and righteousness did R. Akiva offer to his disciples by secretly watching how his master was doing private business in the washroom and then teaching them how to take pants off, what direction to turn the rear, and with which hand to wipe it? When he heard voices protesting his shameful violation of human dignity, R. Akiva proudly replied: "It was a matter of Torah, and I was required to learn it" (Babylonian Talmud, Tractate Berakoth, 62a). It also was permitted for students to secretly enter their master's bedroom and hide under the bed in order to learn how the wise men of Israel made love to their wives under the same pretense that they were "required to learn Torah." The students followed their teacher as best they could, with disastrous consequences as we have seen.

Missing in this relationship was mutual honor between teacher and student—another important principle upheld by the Torah. As it says in the Talmud, "Let your fellow man's honor be as dear to you as your own" (Babylonian Talmud, Avot 2: 10), and "Who is honored? One who honors his fellow human being" (Babylonian Talmud, Avot 4: 1). Just as students are obligated to honor their teacher, a teacher is obligated to honor his students and encourage them. A teacher's responsibility is to care for his students and love them, for they are like sons who bring him pleasure in this world and in the world to come. Our sages declared: "The honor of your students should be as dear to you as your own." As shepherd of his flock, R Akiva should have led his proverbial sheep not in the direction of blindness and ignorance of God's love, but rather in a manner of the great spiritual teachers Hillel and Shamai, Johanan ben Zakkai, Eliezer the Great, Joshua ben Hananiah and many others, who modeled love of the

God of Israel and His divine Torah and brotherly love of others. Otherwise, as Proverbs 14:12 says, "There is a way that seems right to a man, but in the end it leads to death."

R. Akiva was well aware that his generation did not merit the advent of the Messiah and God's Redemption. But, being optimistic by nature, he was convinced that the Jewish people would change to meet the spiritual demands of the Torah, and that the Revolt would be successful in bringing freedom and independence to his people and the Messianic Era to the world. He dreamed that Bar Kokhba would rebuild the Third Temple in Jerusalem after a victorious war against the Romans. He remembered the prophecies of seventy years of Babylonian exile and the rebuilding of the Second Temple. And he knew that seventy years were approaching since the destruction of the Temple in 70CE. After the liberation of Jerusalem, R. Akiva directed Bar Kokhba to begin construction of the Third Temple, a task that could not be completed due to Roman military pressure, internal dissent, and sectarian rivalry. If R. Akiva could have foreseen the grave consequences of the Revolt he initiated and actively supported, he would have prevented it from happening at all. Without enthusiastic support from the religious authorities of the Sanhedrin and Academy, without the spiritual leadership of 'the Father of all Sages' and legions of his disciples and followers, the Bar Kokhba *Revolt would not have been possible and could have been prevented.*

The Opinions of the Rabbis

Not many scholars understand the full ramifications of R. Akiva's responsibilities in the Bar Kokhba Revolt and its grave consequences. The fallout of the failure of the Bar Kokhba Revolt is still with us today. As R. Shlomo Riskin, a contemporary well-known scholar puts it, "For reasons that will probably remain obscure, the students of Rabbi Akiva were not considered by Heaven to have reached the supreme spiritual heights necessary to bring about the Messianic Age."

Speaking of the tragic fate of the 24,000 disciples of R. Akiva, R. Riskin concludes: "Another explanation of their death was that they died in the battlefield when Rabbi Akiva sent them to fight with the Bar Kochba rebellion. And we also see how the beginning of the end of any national uprising or even defensive war is when the people supposedly on the same side deflect their energy away from the enemy and towards their own internal dissensions; this is the causeless hatred which has always caused Israel to miss our chance for redemption!" Such 'causeless hatred' may have contributed toward the failed revolt against Rome. It was also hatred that was responsible for the catastrophe of the First Great Jewish Revolt against the Roman Empire in 66-70 CE.

Many theologians comprehend the colossal effects of R. Akiva's mistake. By proclaiming the wrong man in the wrong time to be the Messiah, and subsequently arousing the Judeans to revolt through military and political battle against the mighty Roman Empire, without approval and support from the Almighty God of Israel, R. Akiva and his 'rabbinic cohort' committed a massive mistake that brought unparalleled historical tragedy to the Jewish people, the consequences of which we still suffer.

Of interest are the insights of the theologian author, R. Samuel, who thinks that out of such tragedy, we can reap some hard-learned lessons. Surely, one of these lessons is to follow rather than 'force' the plan of God: "Talmudic wisdom learned some hard lessons from Jewish history. These lessons may have been directed at all future spiritual and religious *leaders who might attempt to force the hand of God, in forcing the Divine to produce the Messiah.* It may also be seen as a *gentle* reprimand to Rabbi Akiba. Some Jewish thinkers tend to gloss over the consequences of the failed rebellion against Rome, but many people died as a result of Bar Kochba and

Rabbi Akiba. Historically, all human efforts to predict the arrival of the son of David are ultimately doomed to failure. Despite numerous predictions made about his 'alleged arrival'—he has yet to appear and finish the job assigned to him by the prophets." We are in full support of R. Samuel's ideas, even to the point of also issuing a "gentle reprimand" to R. Akiva as has been occasionally delivered in the past by the sages of the Talmud.

Unfortunately, the disciples of R. Akiva failed because they did not rise to the occasion, and instead of the Redemption and the Messianic Age, further catastrophic destruction ensued. As Chabad.org puts it, "These underdeveloped students who have not gathered much Torah knowledge, seek to gain prestige in the eyes of the common people and the inhabitants of their city by jumping to sit at the head of all questions of law and Halakhic judgments in Israel. They spread division, destroy the world, extinguish the light of Torah, and wreak havoc in the vineyard of the God of Hosts. In his wisdom, Solomon alluded to them as follows, (Song of Songs 2:15): "Take for us foxes, little foxes that spoil the vineyards, [our vineyards are blooming]" (Mishnah Torah, chapter 5:4).

While the people must make the effort, it is not their physical strength and human might which brings victories in the Messianic wars and Redemption but the God of Israel. The generation that cannot elevate itself to the heights of love and honor required by God is not worthy of redemption. As R. Yohanan ben Torta says "I do not believe that the Messianic age can begin prior to rectifying the cause of the destruction of the previous Temple" (Yoma 9a).

The State of Jewish Unity

The very same situation concerning Jewish unity (or more appropriately, disunity) exists in our time. In an era when Jews all over the world face rising anti-Semitism, when the delegitimization and destruction of Israel is a goal of the enemies of the Jewish state, when some Jewish fanatics among the Ultra-Orthodox communities embrace furious anti-Semites, causing shame and pain to our people, history appears to be repeating itself. It is more disheartening to see Jews themselves adding to the vilification, especially when it is done in the name of Judaism. For this, there is no justification.

How do statements such as the following, by the True Torah Jews against Zionism, serve the Jewish people: "We American Jews are thankful to be living under the trustworthy government of the United States of America and our honorable President Barack Obama and not under this traitor Netanyahu"? The Ultra-Orthodox Jewish radical sect Neturei Karta, together with many elite intellectuals from universities, members of the press, international activists, human rights protectors, and leftist peace demagogues, both from within the State of Israel and the Diaspora, unite with the Arabs and anti-Semitic elements around the world in their efforts to delegitimize and destroy the Jewish state. They want to live under the Democratic Palestinian Authority. No less, no more. But what do they propose should be done about five and a half million Jews, the Israelis? Well, they answer, Jews will have to ask the lawful Palestinian government's permission to live in their country or even become citizens of the Palestinian state. If they are not allowed to stay (as if there is any doubt!), the Jews must leave the Holy Land and return to the countries of their previous exile (should those countries allow Jews to return), where they are supposed to live peacefully and in harmony with the nations, pray to God "for the welfare of the city" (Jeremiah 29:7), and patiently wait for the coming of the Messiah. Unbelievably, such aims and ambitions make up their official mandate.

A weakened, disunited Jewish nation is easy prey for both anti-Semites and the enemies of Israel. The activities of Neturei Karta—such as collaborating with Palestinians, embracing open enemies of the State of Israel (including racists and Jewish haters), publicly burning the flag of the Jewish State, and demonstrating around the world against the State of Israel and its Government— give the impression that these individuals are seeking a warranty for their future protection and well-being from the Arab world, in the event of Israel's dismantlement or destruction. They do not realize two things: Firstly, Israel cannot be destroyed, because God would not let it happen: ("But Judah shall dwell forever, and Jerusalem from generation to generation" [Joel 3:20]; "They and their children and their children's children will live there forever, and David My servant will be their prince forever" [Ezekiel 37:25]; "I will plant Israel in their own land, never again to be uprooted from the land I have given them" [Amos 9:15].) Secondly, for a new Hitler in the Arab world, be it Ahmadinejad or somebody else from Hamas, Hezbollah, Muslim Brotherhood, Al Qaeda or the Palestinian Authority, the political or ideological allegiances of the Jews in question—whether they be Zionists, Orthodox Torah Jews against Zionists, German patriots or Palestinian collaborators, university and media intellectuals, international activists, Jews from left or right, old or young— make no difference. Like Hitler, they wish to kill all Jews without discrimination.

While anti-Semites place all Jewish people in the same category, the Jews are still divided and fragmented on the basis of politics and religion. There is sectarian rivalry, unresolved animosity within the Torah community, unreasonable hatred, slander and gossip, and lack of love and honor for God and humankind. The tragic lessons of the past, particularly of the first Jewish rebellion and the Bar Kokhba Revolt, have not been learned. As the well known philosopher Santayana says, *"Those who cannot remember the past are condemned to repeat it."* If the Jewish people do not smarten up and bring an end to this state of disunity, the future prospects of the Jewish nation are all doom and gloom.

But we are not without optimism of our own. We believe that our generation will totally repent of its sins and change its ways. At the appointed time God will send the real Messiah, son of David. He will reunite the Ten Tribes of Israel with the rest of the House of Jacob and bring them to the Promised Land to be purified and redeemed. This Messiah chosen by God will not die or be killed until he does everything that has to be done, as perfectly outlined in the Hebrew Bible, the Talmud, and rabbinical literature. Such is God's plan. It also includes building the Third Temple with its sacrificial system and restoring the Land of Israel to its Biblical borders from the River Nile to the River Euphrates. Then, naturally, after a long and happy life, the King Messiah will die, but his son, grandson and the next of kin from his seed (that is, his genealogy) will, if needed, accomplish any remaining unfinished business to meet the spiritual standards of the holy Torah and prepare people everywhere for the world-to-come, the arrival of which is the purpose of all creation.

CHAPTER VI

Rabban Yochanan Ben Zakkai

The Turbulent Times of the First Great Jewish Revolt

The youngest and most distinguished disciple of Rabbi Hillel, Yochanan ben Zakkai inherited his great teacher's peaceful disposition, love for his fellow men, and prophetic wisdom. After the death of Hillel, he became the religious leader of the Jewish nation. During the turbulent years of the First Jewish Revolt against the Romans (66-70AC), R. Yochanan, together with his most prominent disciples, attempted to calm the people in a time of crisis. He urged them to set their weapons aside and negotiate peace with the Romans. In his view, to wage war with the mighty Roman Empire was equivalent to national suicide. Together with the pro-Roman Sadducees and moderate Pharisees, R. Yohanan and the other sages thought that wisdom and pacifism would prevail. Sadly, however, the Zealot fanatics and extremists rejected it all.

When the rebel army under the leadership of the Zealots, John of Giscala and Simon Bar Giora defeated the forces of Cestius Gallus, legate of Syria, at the battle of Beth Horon, their victory boosted the resilience of the rebels. It gave them confidence—or, more accurately, arrogant faith—in ultimate military success over their enemies. But the Romans regrouped. General Vespasian, appointed by Emperor Nero, successfully crushed Jewish resistance in Galilee, Caesarea, and the coastlands. All of the rebels and the civilian population of Judea managed to escape to Jerusalem which became the center of the rebellion. John and Simon, both popular Zealot leaders, desperately started fighting each other for rulership of Jerusalem. Taking part in this battle were Jerusalem's authorities and the fanatical Sikarii of Eleazar ben Simon.

Brutal civil war erupted, which later proved to be disastrous. The rivals not only tried to destroy each other, they also burned their opponents' grain supplies to starve them into submission. The Zealots and Sikarii terrorized the citizens of Jerusalem and fanned the flames of a murderous reign of kidnapping, torture, and robberies; many starved to death, while others tried to run away but were caught by the Romans and crucified, five hundred a day, around the city. Josephus describes the chaos and violence inside Jerusalem in the form of riots, banditry, and fanaticism. The Zealots, together with Sikarii and the criminal elements of Biryonim—all people who would rather die than surrender to the Romans—controlled Jerusalem. Nearly a thousand of them were to find heroic death in the fortress of Masada three years later.

This is how the Talmud describes the situation: "The Biryoni (the Zealot bands who defended Jerusalem) were then in the city. The Rabbis said to them: 'Let us go out and make peace with them [the Romans].' They would not let them, but on the contrary said, 'Let us go out and fight them.' The Rabbis said: 'You will not succeed.' They then rose up and burnt the stores of wheat and barley so that a famine ensued" (Babylonian Talmud, Tractate Gittim, 56a). Clearly, the rebels and their leaders did not listen to R. Yohanan Ben Zakkai and his colleagues. The rabbinical sources indicate twenty-four different factions among the Jews. They did not want to negotiate peace and surrender. Civil war among rival factions raged at full strength. Jerusalem was so war-torn that its citizens had to climb over dead bodies in the Temple to offer their sacrifices. Many thousands of Jews inside the city were dying of famine and plague. A mortal disease afflicted the Jewish people. The rabbis called this disease *sinat chinam,* meaning senseless hatred of one Jew for another Jew.

The Fate of Jerusalem is Sealed

R. Yohanan Ben Zakkai knew that the fate of Jerusalem and the Temple was condemned by Divine Providence. According to the Talmud, for forty years before the destruction of the Second Temple the doors of the *heikhal* (the front part of the Temple building) were locked at night and in the early morning found open. Johanan b. Zakkai said to it: "*Heikhal,* why do you agitate us? We know that you will eventually be destroyed, as it is said [Zechariah 11:1]: 'Open thy doors, O Lebanon, that the fire may devour thy cedars'" (Jerusalem Talmud, Yoma, 6:3, 43c; Babylonian Talmud, Yoma 39b; and see Josephus, Wars, 6:293).

Josephus Flavius also recorded this story: "At the Passover, the eastern gate of the inner temple, being of brass and very firm, and with difficulty shut at eventide by twenty men; moreover with bars strengthened with iron, and having very deep bolts, which went down into the threshold, itself of one stone, was seen at six o'clock at night to open of its own accord. The guards of the temple running told it to the officer, and he, going up, with difficulty closed it. The uninstructed thought this a very favorable sign, that God had opened to them the gate of all goods. But those taught in the divine words, understood that the safety of the temple was removed of itself, and that the gate opened" (Josephus, *Wars of the Jews*, Book VI, Chapter 5:3).

The Prophet Jeremiah gave a detailed account of the Temple's destruction: "For this is what the LORD says about the palace of the king of Judah: "Though you are like Gilead to Me, like the summit of Lebanon, I will surely make you like a desert, like towns not inhabited. I will send destroyers against you, each man with his weapons, and they will cut up your fine cedar beams and throw them into the fire" (Jeremiah 22:6-7). Jeremiah's description offers a precise account of what the Roman soldiers of Titus carried out.

R. Yohanan did what he could to stop the bloody madness unleashed by the Jewish factions in Jerusalem. Not only did they refuse to listen, they even threatened to kill him if he would not stop preaching the surrender of the city. He knew that he had to find a way to escape from Jerusalem as soon as possible in order to negotiate with the Romans to save what was still left—the Sages of the Sanhedrin, scholars of the Torah, and the town of Yavneh.

Heroic Escape

Consider the Talmudic story of R. Yohanan's bold and extremely perilous escape from the fanatical Zealots and doomed Jerusalem. Abba Sikra (literally, Father of the Sikarii, whose real name was Ben Batiah), the head of the *Biryonim*, the extremist Jewish militants, was the brother-in-law of Rabban Yochanan ben Zakkai [in other sources he is presented as the nephew of Yohanan ben Zakkai]. Ben Zakkai sent a message to Abba Sikra inviting him to a secret meeting, to which he went. Once together, Rabban Yochanan asked him, "How long will you carry on like this, and starve everyone to death?" Abba Sikra responded, "What can I do? The situation is out of my control. If I tell them anything adverse, they will kill me," to which R. Yochanan instructed him: "Devise a plan that will enable me to leave. Perhaps something can still be saved." Abba Sikra then arrived at the following plot: "Pretend that you are ill, and everyone will come to visit you. Then bring some stinking object and place it next to you and they'll say that you have died. Have your disciples carry you for burial outside the city."

With his students Rabbi Eliezer and Rabbi Yehoshua acting as pall-bearers, the coffin approached the Biryoni-manned guard-post just within the wall of Yerushalayim. The guards wanted to plunge their swords into the coffin to make sure that they were not being tricked, but the students said, "The Romans will say that they're stabbing their leader!" The guards then wanted to push the coffin hard, to see if anyone inside would cry out. Again, the students quick-wittedly told them that if they did that, the hated Romans would say, "The Jews are pushing the body of their leader!" The Biryoni guard opened the gate and reluctantly let the small burial party through" (Babylonian Talmud, Tractate Gittim, 56a).

According to a well-known Jewish tradition, priests must be buried outside the city wall. Feigned burial was therefore R. Yohanan's only means of escape, but it was clearly something the Zealots at the gates had thought of, so they routinely checked bodies to make sure they were not escapees. Thankfully, on account of the intervention of Abba Sikra, their leader, R. Yohanan, together with R. Eliezer and R. Joshua, was saved.

'Peace be Unto You, O King!'

Finally, the burial procession safely arrived to their destination, the Roman headquarters: "When the Jewish party reached the Roman camp, Rabban Yochanan ben Zakkai emerged from the coffin and greeted the general, 'Peace be unto you, O King! Peace be unto you, O King!' To which Vespasian responded, 'You have incurred the death penalty twice. First, you have called me King, and I am not the King! Second, if I am indeed the King, why have you not come out to me earlier, to how me proper respect?'

Ben Zakkai answered, 'I knew you had to be a king, because our prophets have foretold that the Temple will fall only into the hands of a king. And the reason I have not come out to you until now is that we are plagued by violent extremists within the city, who would not let me come out!'"

Here is another version of Rabban Yohanan ben Zakkai's response to Vespasian: "That which you have said, 'I am not the king,' certainly you are a king! If you were not a king, Jerusalem would not have been given into your hands. For it is written, 'And Lebanon by a mighty one will fall'" (Isaiah 10:34; T. Bab. Gittin, fol. 56b; Midrash Echa Rabbati, 46. 4). With this explanation R. Yohanan let Vespasian know that he was defeating the Jewish rebels, not their God who had reduced the Roman Emperor to merely an actor in this long foretold tragedy: "A mighty one is none other than a king, for it is written, 'their mighty one shall be of themselves and its ruler shall go out from its midst'" (Jer. 30:21). And Lebanon is none other than the Temple, for it is said, 'This good mountain and the Lebanon'" (Deuteronomy 3:25).

Vespasian responded, "If there were a snake curled around a barrel of honey, would you not break the barrel (that is, set fire to the walls of the city) in order to get rid of the snake?" Rabban Yochanan ben Zakkai was not able to respond to this. (At this point, Rabbi Yosef, and some say Rabbi Akiva, commented that sometimes 'G-d makes the wise foolish; for Ben Zakkai should have responded that he had hoped to defeat the militants without having to destroy the walls of the city, and then to make peace with the Romans'). At this point, an Imperial messenger arrived from Rome, and announced, 'Arise! For the Emperor has died and the Senators have decided to make Vespasian, General of the Legions of Rome, the new Emperor'" (Babylonian Talmud, Tractate Gittim, 56b)!

The Bargain between R. Yohanan
and Emperor Vespasian

The Talmudic dialogue between the Emperor Vespasian and R. Yohanan continues: "Vespasian said to Rabban Yochanan, 'I will leave now, to return to Rome. But I will dispatch someone to take my place. Before I go, ben Zakkai, you may make a request, which I will grant you.' R. Yohanan said to Vespasian: 'Give me Yavneh and her sages, the descendants of Rabban Gamliel, and a cure to heal Rabbi Tzadok. Allow me to continue to survive in Yavneh with a Sanhedrin, and I will relinquish national sovereignty in Jerusalem.' Here again, Rabbi Yosef, and some say Rabbi Akiva, comment that sometimes 'G-d makes the wise foolish;' for Ben Zakkai should have requested the preservation of Jerusalem and the Holy Temple, and that the Jewish People should be given a second chance to prove their loyalty to Rome'" (Babylonian Talmud, Gittin 56b).

There are many authors producing different versions of this story, each with its own particular variations, especially regarding the account of the negotiation between R. Yohanan and Emperor Vespasian. According to their versions, Vespasian presented R. Yohanan with three options—one of which was the saving of Jerusalem and the Holy Temple—and gave him the choice of one as his reward. The veracity of this account is very doubtful. The Emperor could not have made such an offer. He knew very well that the Jewish rebels had killed too many Roman soldiers and caused excessive physical, moral, and political damage to the Empire. The Jews did not surrender the city and desperately fought to the death. The victorious Romans could not have possibly rewarded this nation by sparing them Jerusalem and the Temple, for they understood their rich symbolic value for the Jewish people as powerful emblems of national pride and strength. Rather, the Romans' intention was to punish the rebellious Jews in such a manner that would undermine the spirit of this tiny nation once and for all and also deliver a powerful lesson to other nations under Roman domination.

Their terrible means and methods—destroying the city and Temple, plowing over Jerusalem, killing one million and one hundred thousand Jews and selling the rest to slavery—were more appropriate to the Romans, and served as cautionary warning to other nations that might rebel against the mighty Empire. Besides, both R. Yochanan and the Emperor were aware that the fate of the Temple and Jerusalem had been determined by the Prophets of God. Nobody could have prevented the Divine ordinance. (R. Yohanan had explained the prophecies to Emperor Vespasian, so that he too knew prophecies of the imminent destruction of the city and Temple). Even the Talmud, in defense of Rabban Yohanan ben Zakkai, explains his thinking; namely, that events in the war had gone too far for such a request to be honored. In order, therefore, to preserve the Torah and save the rest of the Jewish people, R. Yohanan had to insist on choosing Yavneh and its sages. Being impressed with his prediction, to say nothing of his wisdom and spirit of peace towards the Romans, Emperor Vespasian might have granted his request to save Sanhedrin and the Torah scholars in the town of Yavneh because it was reported that these sages did not support the rebellion and were inclined to make peace with the Romans. But the notion that Vespasian committed to saving Jerusalem and the Holy Temple as a reward (and for what actions it is not clear) confounds all common sense.

A Bitter Dispute between R. Akiva and R. Yohanan

This said, it is surprising to read R. Akiva's groundless criticism of the R. Yohanan ben Zakkai's decision to choose Yavneh, the Sages of the Sanhedrin and Torah scholars instead of Jerusalem and the Temple. We have already drawn attention to passages from Scripture that demonstrate that the destruction of Jerusalem and the Holy Temple was God's will given the many sins of the people (Jeremiah 22:6-7; Zechariah 11:1). Here, however, is more Biblical evidence:

"I will bring an end to the sounds of joy and gladness and to the voices of bride and bridegroom in the towns of Judah and the streets of Jerusalem, for the land will become desolate" (Jeremiah 7:34). The prophet Micah gave staggering description of the utter destruction of Jerusalem and the Temple: "Therefore because of you, Zion will be plowed like a field, Jerusalem will become a heap of rubble, the temple hill a mound overgrown with thickets" (3:12). The prophecy of Daniel confirms the words of R. Yohanan that it will be 'the prince' (the king) who will be victorious over the Jews: "And the people of the prince that shall come shall destroy the city and the sanctuary; and the end thereof shall be with a flood, and unto the end of the war desolations are determined" (Daniel 9:26).

It is impossible to believe that R. Akiva was not familiar with these prophesied passages and the real historical situation of the First Great Jewish Revolt. He was a mature man by this time and had witnessed the fall-out of this tragedy. Why, then, was he not happy with the choice that R. Yohanan had made at the famous meeting with Vespasian? The outcome of this meeting had been very significant for the Jewish people and Judaism. His discontent and displeasure with R. Yohanan's decision is amply expressed in his damning indictments: "God makes the wise foolish," "God sometimes turns wise people backward, and transforms their wisdom into foolishness" (B. T. Gittin 57b), and "He turns wise men [i.e. the sages] backward and confuses their mind" (Isaiah 44:25). R. Akiva's caustic attitude immediately reminds us of the shepherd Akiva who in his ignorance and blind hatred towards Torah scholars claimed to want "to bite them so badly as to crush their bones."

Here we have two great giants of the Torah, two pillars of Judaism, two different personalities who disagree on the most important question in Jewish religion: Can the Jewish people survive without the Holy Temple and its sacrificial system? R. Yohanan's response was an emphatic "Yes," and he chose to save what was realistically possible (i.e. the sages of the Sanhedrin, the Torah scholars, and the town of Yavneh). It has been proven through two thousand years of Jewish history that Judaism can survive and even flourish without the Temple and its sacrifices. And as we read in Scripture, God says, "For I desire mercy, and not sacrifice; and the knowledge of God more than burnt offerings" (Hosea 6:6). The same perspective was expressed by the prophet Isaiah: "The multitude of your sacrifices— what are they to Me" (1:11)?

R. Yohanan preferred the destruction of Jerusalem and the Temple with its sacrifices to potentially risking the survival of the Jewish people. Time has confirmed the excellence of his choice. Surely he knew that "To do what is right and just is more acceptable to the LORD than sacrifice" (Proverbs 21:3). His foresight and wisdom give him the strength and courage to reassure his disciple of the future restoration of Israel: "Once when R. Johanan b. Zakkai was leaving Jerusalem, R. Joshua was walking behind him and saw the Temple in ruins. R. Joshua said, 'Woe is us that this has been destroyed, the place where atonement was made for the sins of Israel.' 'No, my son, do you not know that we have a means of making atonement that is like it? And what is it? It is deeds of love, as it is said [Hosea 6:6]: 'For I desire kindness and not sacrifice'" (Aboth Rabbi Nathan 4, 21).

R. Yohanan taught that the loss of the Temple would not be permanent. The people of Israel would repent, and God, in due time, would send the Messiah who would build the Temple and reinstate the sacrificial system. There will be a reunification of all the Tribes of the House of Israel who will return to the Promised Land. The whole of Israel will be redeemed during the

Messianic Age, which will be followed by the purely spiritual World-To-Come.

Peace and War

R. Yohanan taught that the redemption will be initiated by the Almighty. All attempts by the Jewish people to redeem themselves had failed because they had come through human initiative. If the Jews had been obedient to God there would have been no destruction. The Messianic World also has to be initiated by God, not by the people. In waiting for its arrival, the Jewish people must exercise patience. All their efforts should be directed at establishing a proper spiritual relationship with God and others. Only through repentance, prayer, and obedience to God and observance of His divine laws will Israel give rise to the generation that merits Redemption. Messianic speculations initiated by individuals, whether they are religious, political, or military leaders of the nation, do not serve any good, and as the history of the Jewish nation shows, these human efforts have always ended in catastrophic disaster.

Unfortunately, in the First Great Revolt against the Romans the Jews could not overcome the national sins of baseless hatred, factional rivalry, and religious fanaticism. The chaos, bloody terror, and madness of the Zealots and Sikarii prevailed. Because of these sins, the Revolt was crushed, masses of Jews were killed, and Jerusalem and the Temple were destroyed as God's punishment to a sinful nation. R. Yohanan fully appreciated the historical and religious reality in the world and particularly Judaea. He knew the strength and might of the Roman Empire and the rebels' negligible prospects of success. He was perfectly aware that for Jews to merit God's redemption, the nation must totally repent of its sins, and obey God and His Laws, as it is written: "Does the LORD delight in burnt offerings and sacrifices as much as in obeying the voice of the LORD? To obey is better than sacrifice, and to heed is better than the fat of rams" (1 Samuel 15:22). And elsewhere: "He has showed you, O man, what is good. And what does the LORD require of you? To act justly and to love mercy and to walk humbly with your God" (Micah 6:8).

In this revolt God was not on the side of the rebels. Consequently, the rebels, Jerusalem, and the Holy Temple were inevitably destined for slaughter, slavery, and destruction. But what is important, and has proven itself throughout a long period of exile, is Rabban Yohanan ben Zakkai's vision of the survival of the Jewish people and their religion without the Holy Temple and its sacrificial system and even without possession of the Land of Israel. Judaism of today is the most powerful testimony to the rightness of R. Yohanan's decision at his famous historical meeting with Vespasian. That meeting determined the fate and destiny of the Jewish people.

R. Akiva vehemently objected R. Yohanan's decision to choose Yavneh and its sages instead of trying to save the Temple. The validity of his criticism is very dubious. R. Akiva was the most influential Torah scholar and the religious leader of his time. It is he who took upon himself the heavy burden of reshaping the Jewish religion after the destruction of the Temple under Roman occupation—a task he took from the hands of Rabban Yohanan ben Zakkai. The destruction of the Temple was a tragedy for the Jewish people and caused a major crisis in Judaism. It was R. Akiva with his five closest disciples who faced a new reality of worshiping the God of Israel without His sanctuary and everyday sacrificial rituals, to which Jews had been accustomed for centuries. These great men developed, refined, and elevated rabbinical Judaism to unseen spiritual heights, from worship centered around the Temple in Jerusalem, where atonement for sin was possible through sacrificial rituals, to the forgiveness of sin achieved through repentance, prayer, Torah study, and acts of love and kindness. They taught the Jewish people that even without the Temple and its sacrificial system, the God of Israel has not abandoned His people. He still loves and cares for them and wants all of them to merit life in the World-to-Come. The classical rabbinical Judaism of these men outlived the greatest Empires and their idolatrous religions in spite of all the bloody persecutions and Holocausts. Judaism has emerged from two thousand years of exile as a resilient, adaptable, portable, and purified monotheistic religion with the highest moral and spiritual values humanity has ever witnessed.

Surely R. Akiva was aware of the events of the First Jewish-Roman War and the intention of the Romans to destroy Jerusalem and the Holy Temple. Certainly, he knew the prophetic predictions of the fate of the city and sanctuary, as the Talmudic story of Mount Scopus reveals. According to the story, upon reaching the Temple Mount during a walk towards Jerusalem, R. Gamaliel, R. Elazar, R. Joshua, and R. Akiva saw a fox emerging from the place of the Holy of Holies. With the exception of R. Akiva, who laughed, they began weeping. To their question, "Why are you laughing?" he responded by asking, "Why are you weeping?" They answered: "A place [so holy] that it is said of it, 'the stranger that approaches it shall die' (Numbers 1:51), and now foxes traverse it, and we should not weep?'" "That is why I laugh," R. Akiva said, "for it is written, 'I shall have bear witness for My faithful witnesses, Uriah the Priest and Zechariah the son of Jeberechiah'" (Isaiah 8:2). "Now what is the connection between Uriah and Zechariah? Uriah was in the time of the First Temple, and Zechariah was in the time of the Second Temple! But the Torah makes Zachariah's prophecy dependent upon Uriah's prophecy. Of Uriah, it is written: 'Therefore, because of you, Zion shall be plowed as a field; Jerusalem shall become heaps, and the Temple Mount like the high places of a forest'" (Micah 3:12). "Of

Zachariah, it is written, continues R. Akiva, "Old men and women shall yet sit in the streets of Jerusalem (Zechariah 8:4). And so, Akiva defended his position thus, "As long as Uriah's prophecy had not been fulfilled, I feared that Zechariah's prophecy may not be fulfilled either. But now that Uriah's prophecy has been fulfilled, it is certain that Zechariah's prophecy will be fulfilled." With these words they replied to him: "Akiva, you have consoled us! Akiva, you have consoled us!" (Talmud, Makkot 24b).

When R. Akiva saw the ruins of the Temple in fulfillment of the prophecies of Jeremiah (7:34; 22:6-7; Daniel 9:26; Zechariah 11:1; Micah 3:12), with which he was very familiar, he immediately recalled the prophecies of the rebuilding of the Third Temple and the restoration of Israel: "Jerusalem will be a city without walls because of the great number of men and livestock in it" (Zechariah 2:4). The prophets throughout the Scripture reinforce the belief that the God of Israel will make Jerusalem a magnificent, peaceful, and prosperous city, where "old men and old women dwell in the street of Jerusalem, and maidens and young men dance with gladness. I will give them comfort and joy instead of sorrow" (Zechariah 8:4; Jeremiah 31:13).

In the light of these Scriptural passages, it is highly improbable that R. Akiva criticized R Yohanan for his decision to choose Yavneh and the sages instead of the Holy Temple, as such a choice, or any kind of option for that matter, was simply unavailable. R. Akiva knew that Jerusalem and the Holy Temple were destined for destruction and there was no chance to save them. There was no justification for R. Akiva's censure of his teacher because such criticism would indeed involve a form of self-criticism. As our sages say, "there is no greater honor than that due a teacher, and no greater awe than that due a teacher" (Avot 4:15). In Judaism, criticizing one's teacher is considered the equivalent of criticizing the Divine Presence, as implied in this passage: "And the people spoke out against God and Moses" (Numbers 21:5). Furthermore,

R. Akiva followed R. Yohanan in teaching his followers the same doctrines: studying the Torah, obeying God's Commandments, and performing good deeds were the only means of survival for Judaism and the Jewish people in the religious-political environment after destruction of the Temple and harsh subjugation of the Imperial Rome.

Here is an illustration in point: R. Akiva told the parable of the fox passing by the river that saw fish desperately swimming to escape the hooks and nets of fishermen. When the fox suggested that they come up on dry land to escape this danger, they replied that it is not smart thing for us to do. If we are in danger while we are in the water which is our natural habitat, what chance do we have of survival if we leave the water? R. Akiva remarked that so it is with the Jewish people. In our condition, when we sit and study the Torah, of which it is written that this is our life and the length of our days, if we neglect it, how much worse off we shall be! He went on to compare the Torah for Jews to water for fish, with the implication that abandoning the Torah would be a greater danger to survival (Mesechta Berachot 61b).

"Why do You Weep?"

The so-called 'bitter' dispute between R. Yochanan and R. Akiva has been a matter of obsession for many theological writers. But there was, indeed, no dispute to begin with. As a matter of fact, there were no disputes at all because by the time (many decades or even centuries after the destruction of Jerusalem and the Holy Temple) the Talmudic story was written R. Yochanan ben Zakkai had been long dead.

Despite this, many scholars have gone so far as to assert that at the time of his death R. Yohanan was tormented with agonizing doubts about the rightness of his decision. While there is no way of knowing with certainty whether R. Yohanan ever regretted his decision, these scholars have insisted that a clue can be found in the story of his death. When R. Yohanan lay ailing, his disciples came to visit him. Seeing them, he began to cry. They asked, "Light of Israel, pillar of the Torah, strong hammer—why do you weep?" He replied, "There are two paths open before me—one leading to paradise and one to hell, and I do not know by which of them they are taking me—should I not weep?"

Did R. Yohanan tell his disciples that he was weeping because of the decision he made at the meeting with Vespasian? Does Scripture or any other source offer any indication that this was the case? Not at all! Why then are there so many speculations, baseless assumptions, and fantasies? Could it not be that R. Yohanan had another reason to weep before his death? As is said in the Gemara (Sanhedrin 101a) R. Akiva said to R. Eliezer, "The Rebbi taught that 'there is no righteous person in the land who did good and did not sin'" (Kohelet 7:20). The same idea is conveyed in Ecclesiastes: "For there is no righteous man on earth who does good and sins not" (7:20). Like any righteous man, R. Yohanan could have sinned and was not sure in his last hour if God had forgiven him. What was his sin, and why he was tormented? No one has the key with which to unlock this mystery. He kept the source of his anguish deep inside and took it with him to eternity. This explanation is more viable than the previous one and justifies his doubts about his destiny after death. We are certain that for all of his heroic efforts to save Judaism and the Jewish People—as manifested in his teaching of the Torah and upbringing of a new generation of remarkably outstanding scholars—Rabban Yohanan ben Zakkai now lives with God. As his eulogy proclaimed, "Not even the guard of the gate of Gehinom could stand in his way!"

R. Yohanan suffered a heavy heart at the fall of Jerusalem and the Holy Temple. Yet he did more than anyone else to save

Judaism and the Jewish people and paved the way for Israel to rise again. The date of R. Yochanan's death is unknown, but the esteem of future generations for his life and work is expressed in the Mishnaic statement that "When R. Yohanan b. Zakkai died, the luster of wisdom ceased" (Sotah 9:15).

The Messianic World and the Vision of R. Akiva

Now let us focus on R. Akiva's role in the Second Jewish Revolt of 132 to135CE. Whereas R. Yochanan was a pacifist unsupportive of the military struggle against the Romans who tried to negotiate peace, R. Akiva, by contrast, was not a man of peace but a man of action. As a nationalistic Jew who hated the Roman occupation with its influx of idolatrous beliefs, he dreamed of a free and independent Judaea where Jews would be preoccupied with the study of the Torah while existing in a state of peace, justice, and harmony with God and others. His vision of the Messiah and the Messianic World was not associated with the distant future. He fully expected that the recapturing of Jerusalem, rebuilding of the Third Temple, reinstatement of the sacrificial system, and, in short, the realization the long-awaited Messianic Era, would unfold during his life time. As the *Jewish Encyclopedia* mentions, for R. Akiva, the Messianic Age was limited to forty years as was the reign of David and Solomon—a notion that completely contradicts the commonly accepted concept of Millennium (Midrash Teh. 90:15).

The gathering of the exiles, or *kibbuzgaliyyot* in Hebrew (primarily the Lost Ten Tribes of Israel), was not the priority of the R. Akiva's messiah, since he maintained that they were lost forever and would never return. "To the future world," he said, "all Israel will be admitted, with the exception of the generation of the wilderness and the Ten 'lost' Tribes" (Sanhedrin 11:3 and 110b).

This view was in direct contrast to the Tanakh, Talmud, and rabbinical literature (Deuteronomy 30:3; Isaiah 11:12; 27:13; 35:8; 49:22; 60:4-9; 66:20; Micah 4:6; 7:11; Ezekiel 39:27; Zechariah 11:10-12; Apoc. Abraham 31; II Ezra 13:13; Baruch 4:37). As we read in various sources, "In the days of the Messiah the Ten Tribes will be miraculously brought back across the mighty waters of the Euphrates River" (II Ezra 13:39-47; Syriac Apoc. Baruch 77; Sanhedrin 10:13).

R. Riskin characterizes R. Akiva's beliefs this way: "Rabbi Akiva believed differently. He understood the function of the Holy Temple and Jerusalem as being cardinal to the mission of Israel, a holy nation and a kingdom of priest-teachers (to the world) through whom all of the families of the earth are to be blessed."

Here is the interesting point. Scriptural passages such as the following do not speak exclusively of the Jewish People: "You only have I chosen of all the families of the earth" (Amos 3:2); or "For you are a people holy to the Lord your God. For the Lord your God has chosen you out of all peoples on the face of the earth to be His People, His treasured possession" (Deuteronomy 7:6). Make no mistake: God speaks here of the genuine nation of the whole Twelve Tribes of Israel, not of Judah alone, not of a Christian 'spiritual Israel,' nor the nation of Muslims, nor any other nations who try to single-handedly replace the authentic Israel. God clearly states, "Israel has been chosen out of all people on the face of the earth."

How could R. Akiva's vision come to pass, if he excluded the 'lost' Ten Tribes of Israel from the future Messianic Age and the World-to-Come? Many Biblical scholars and theologians have written on the subject of Israel's specialness as a 'Nation of Priests' and a 'Light to the World.' Much valuable research has been poured into the numerous books and articles that have been produced on the subject. Allow us to humbly add a few considerations to this body of scholarship. First of all, let us raise some fundamental questions: Has Israel fulfilled its divine mission? Has it become 'a Covenant for the people and a Light for the Gentiles'? Has it brought God's salvation to the ends of the earth? Clearly, the answer to these questions is an unequivocal 'No.' Why is this so? Because the time has not arrived yet for Israel to do what the Almighty has designated them to do. At the present time the Israelites of the Ten Tribes in exile cannot truly be called 'Israelites' in the precise, religious sense because of their lives and faiths. Rather, they are Gentiles, properly speaking, as they are not cognizant of their Israelite origins. To paraphrase from Scripture, they have mingled with godless foreigners: "Like a woman unfaithful to her husband, so you have been unfaithful to me, O house of Israel," declares the LORD (Jeremiah 3:20).

Can today's 'Israelites' constitute a 'Nation of Priests' and bring the glory of the God of Israel to the ends of the earth? No matter what the answer to this question, hundreds of millions of 'Israelites' from the Ten Tribes *will* acknowledge their Israelite identity. How do we know that? Because the Scripture says so! As the Bible asserts, they will return to the God of their fathers, and He will acknowledge and accept them: "In the place where it was said to them, 'You are not My people,' it will be said 'You are the sons of the living God'" (Hosea 1:10). With splendid poetical skill, Isaiah prophesied of the future redemption of Israel by Almighty: "Sing for joy, O heavens, for the LORD has done this; shout aloud, O earth beneath. Burst into song, you mountains, you forests and all your trees, for the LORD has redeemed Jacob, he will display His glory in Israel" (44:23).

Such redemption will take place in the 'Latter Days,' at the dawn of the Messianic Era, and will be possible with the help of the Jewish nation, the keepers of the Law (Yalkut Shimeoni, Song of Solomon 905 on Jeremiah 3:18), "For Torah will go forth from Zion, and the word of the Lord from Jerusalem" (cf. Isaiah 2:3; Micah 4:2); the Prophet Elijah (Malachi 4:5-6) will turn the hearts of the fathers to their children, and the hearts of the children to their fathers; at the advent of the Messiah, the King of Israel (Ezekiel 37:22).

To accomplish their unique mission, the Houses of Judah and Israel must repent and reunite, the Messiah must be revealed, the Messianic World must begin, and Israel must be redeemed. When the numerous Biblical prophecies of reunion and the Messianic Age come to pass, and Israel will become one nation as it was in the time of Moses; only then will Israel reach the heights of God's wisdom and perfection, overcome the limitations of the physical world, and experience redemption as it is transformed into a Nation of Priests and a Light to the World. Only in the time of the Messianic Era will the house of Israel finally know its God (Ezekiel 39:22, 28-29), become a rout to Salvation for the Gentiles, and fulfill their divine destiny. God says of Israel: "I will bless those who bless you and whoever curses you I will curse; and all peoples on earth will be blessed through you" (Genesis 12:31). This ancient prophecy will find its complete fulfillment only in the Messianic Time. Because of the Israelites and through them, the Almighty will bless all the people of the world. Of this period of future history, it has been said: "At this stage, when it becomes possible to observe the Torah and its *mitzvoth* in their totality, the era of the Messiah will have actually begun" (Maimonides, Laws of Kings and Wars 11:4).

Let us return to the protagonist of our narrative. R. Akiva directed all of his energy, ideas, influence, and indeed life towards achieving his vision. Unlike R. Yohanan, who believed that redemption must be initiated by the Almighty and only upon the achievement of certain conditions, by his own authority R. Akiva ignited the flame of Revolt against the Romans. R. Yohanan warned that any human effort to initiate the redemption and the coming of the Messiah would lead to catastrophe. As for R. Akiva, many contemporary sages, colleagues, and even his closest disciples (R. Joshua, Yochai, father of Simon, R. Eliezer from Modiin, R. Tarfon, and R. Judah) advised him not to take part in the armed Revolt and not to declare its military leader, Bar Kokhba, the Messiah. They warned him of the great responsibility of deep involvement in political Messianism and the profound consequences of potential failure for the Jewish people. No one and nothing could change R. Akiva's fierce determination to proceed with armed confrontation against the Roman Empire and the proclamation of Bar Kokhba as the Jewish Messiah. R. Akiva underestimated the political situation in the Roman World and particularly Judaea. He undervalued the lack of moral and spiritual readiness among his 24,000 students and the Jewish people of his generation for redemption and the Messianic Age. He gave up on the Ten Tribes of Israel in exile, saying that they were lost forever and would never return to the Promised Land. How can one speak of the redemption of the whole House of Israel in the days of Mashiach without the Ten Tribes? In his sincere hope and belief that a well-planned and organized rebellion would be successful, R. Akiva boldly tried to force Divine Providence to accord with his vision of final victory over the Romans and the arrival of the blessed Messianic Age. It is not the Jewish people who wage and win Messianic Wars, however, but God. The Bar Kokhba Revolt was brutally crushed and so were the dreams and aspirations of R. Akiva.

R. Akiva died a hero by means of a torturous cruel death. Executed by the Romans on the eve of *Yom Kippur* in the city of Caesarea, with his last breath he recited *Shema*: "Hear, O Israel, God is our God; God is One." A heavenly voice (*a bath kol*) went out and announced: "Blessed are you, Rabbi Akiva that your life expired with '*Echad*' [i.e. One]." The ministering Angels said before the Holy One, Blessed be He: "Such Torah, and such a reward?" He replied to them: "Their portion is in life." A heavenly voice went forth and proclaimed, "Happy art thou, R. Akiva, that thou art destined for the life of the World-to-Come" (Babylonian Talmud, Berachot 61b).

CHAPTER VII

Rabbi Eliezer ben Hyrcanus and Rabbi Akiva

"I have never taught anything that I had not learned from my masters" (Sukkah 28a).

The most prominent disciple of Rabbi Yohanan ben Zakkai, who realized his enormous potential and characterized him as "a cemented cistern that loses not a drop of water" (Pirkei Avot 2:8), Rabbi Eliezer ben Hyrcanus was a great Tanna active during the last quarter of the first century and at the turn of the second century. The sixth most frequently mentioned sage in the Mishnah, his respect and devotion to his teachers are embodied in his famous saying: "I have never taught anything that I had not learned from my masters" (Sukkah 28a). R. Eliezer was a member of the Sanhedrin under the presidency of Gamaliel II. He established his own academy in Lydda where he taught many disciples, including R. Akiva. Officially he became known as 'Eliezer *ha-Gadol'* (the Great) but was generally addressed simply as 'Rabbi Eliezer.' Of his greatness as a scholar and sage, Rabbi Yohanan said that, "If all the sages of Israel were on one scale of the balance and Rabbi Eliezer ben Hyrcanus on the other scale, he would outweigh them all" (Mishnah, Pirkei Avot 2:8). His honesty and judicial impartiality was illustrated from the Biblical passage, "That which is altogether just shalt thou follow" (Deuteronomy 16:20), and this was explained as "Seek a reliable court: Go after R. Eliezer to Lydda or after Johanan ben Zakkai to Beror Hel" (Sanhedrin 32b).

R. Eliezer's ideas and approaches provide a fascinating counterpoint to R. Akiva. His interpretation of Scripture was quite conservative. He strictly followed established authoritative traditions in religious practice and upheld the teaching of his highly respected masters. But as his most renowned student, R. Akiva (Yer. Pesachim VI. 33b) viciously opposed R. Eliezer's 'old-fashioned' method of interpretation. In introducing a more creative and dynamic approach—by means of which he was able "to discover things that were even unknown to Moses"—R. Akiva sparked an ideological battle between conservatism and modernity that reflected the historical situation of the Jewish nation after the destruction of the Second Temple. R. Eliezer and his conservative followers defended the 'original intent' of the Torah of Moses and taught that in order to preserve the Torah and Oral Law, they would have to strictly uphold the teachings and traditions of the previous generations and their sages. R. Akiva and his close circle of disciples preferred a new creative approach, claiming that times had changed and innovation was necessary for Judaism to survive in a modern historical-religious environment.

The Heroism of R. Akiva and R. Eliezer

Comparisons of R. Eliezer and R. Akiva frequently praise both scholars for their reputed humility and courage. In juxtaposing the two scholars, R. Tzvi Freman, for example, characterizes R. Akiva as a self-effacing yet heroic personality for inciting and leading the Bar Kokhba Revolt: "Rabbi Eliezer ben Hyrkanus was known for his humility; he would never say a word of Torah that he did not hear from his teacher, yet he was in constant altercation with his colleagues and stood his ground to the end. The same with Rabbi Akiva, who was so humble he sat in a class of small children at the age of forty—and yet stood in fearless rebellion against the awesome Roman Empire" (R. Tzvi Freman, Chabad).

Time and again, R. Akiva is characterized as a humble, fearless, and heroic personality (which he truly was) for inciting and leading the Bar Kokhba Revolt against "the awesome Roman Empire." But only a few thinkers (such as R. Hai Gaon, R. Pinchas Stolper, R. Dovid Rosenfeld, R. Michael Leo Samuel, R Shlomo Riskin and some others) have had the mettle to explain the serious implication of his approach for the Jewish people: the merciless massive slaughter of the Jews, the loss of the land of Israel, and two thousand years of exile with unprecedented suffering and persecution. This great tragedy could have been prevented if R. Akiva and his colleagues had acted in the manner of responsible peacemakers such as R. Hillel, Rabban Gamliel, R.Yohanan ben Zakkai, R. Judah, and R. Joshua. While R. Akiva may have been a humble man, to praise him for fearlessness and heroism in connection with the Jewish Revolt, which he organized, ignited, and led together with the military leader Bar Kokhba, is to ignore his immense responsibility for its tragic consequences.

The Romans executed many great rabbis in the aftermath of the crushed Bar Kokhba Revolt, a number of whom were not necessarily guilty of taking an active part in the Revolt. Most of them were sentenced to cruel deaths for violating the Roman laws directed against teaching and possessing the Torah, circumcision, public gatherings, and the practice of Judaism in general. All of them displayed courage and heroism, preferring torment and death to renouncing the religion of their fathers and faith in the God of Israel.

The Talmud offers a moving account of the execution of R. Hanina ben Teradion, one of the ten martyrs executed in the time of Emperor Hadrian by being burnt at the stake. The Romans arrested R. Hanina ben Teradion for the possessing of the Torah and teaching it in public gatherings. Right away they brought him for execution, wrapped the scroll of the Torah around him, and set him on fire. But fast death of the sage was not in mind of the persecutors. They wanted to see a long suffering and agony as satisfying punishment for violating the Romans' laws. They soaked tufts of wool in water, and placed them over his heart, for him not to die quickly. His daughter burst out sobbing, "Father, that I should see you in this state!" R. Hanina replied, "If it were I alone being burnt it would have been a thing hard to bear; but now that I am burning together with the Scroll of the Law, He who will have regard for the plight of the Torah will also have regard for my plight." These words touched the heart of the Executioner, "Rabbi, if I raise the flame and take away the tufts of wool from over thy heart, will thou cause me to enter into the life to come?" After R. Hanina answered and swore to him that it will be so, the Executioner jumped into the fire. Immediately the Heavenly voice was heard saying that R. Hananiah ben Teradion and the Executioner have been assigned to the world to come. When Rabbi Yehuda HaNasi heard it he wept and said: "One person may acquire eternal life in a single moment, for another only after many years" (Babylonian Talmud, Tractate Abodah Zarah, folio 18a).

In the manner of these great men, R. Eliezer modeled a life of authentic heroism and courage. Let us not forget the story of his dramatic rescue of his beloved Master Rabban Yohanan ben Zakkai. Together with his well-known colleague R. Joshua, he saved his teacher's life by smuggling him—in a coffin, no less—away from the hands of the fanatics and terrorists. At great peril to his own life, R. Eliezer ensured the survival of ben Zakkai. Because of the determination and heroism of these three men, the survival of the Academy of Yavneh, sages, and even Judaism was made possible. R. Eliezer was not a sage who sacrificed his own principles to conciliate the majority, but one who would have fought to the death on their behalf. Perhaps there is no better example of his integrity than his trial before the Sanhedrin.

The Trial of R. Eliezer: The Majority Rules

Let the honor of your fellow be as dear to you as your own" (Mishnah, Pirkei Avot 2:19).

A particular oven in R. Eliezer's day was the source of much contention. The majority of sages claimed that the Aknai oven, as it was called—a vessel consisting of tiles separated from one another by sand (and resembling a 'coiled snake') but externally plastered over with cement—was susceptible to Levitical impurity. Never afraid to counter majority opinion, R. Eliezer openly contested their claim, asserting that such an oven is always pure because it is not considered a proper vessel. The heated discussion turned into a vicious debate that pitted R. Eliezer against his colleagues.

On the morning of the Sanhedrin dispute R. Eliezer and his disciple R. Akiva discussed the upcoming trial as they walked together to the Academy of Yavneh. "Master," said R. Akiva, "the issue has been clearly defined. The oven is ritually pure. Unfortunately, the other Sages do not agree with your interpretation." R. Eliezer replied: "Akiva, you have stated the problem well, but what is the answer? My colleagues have not understood the underlying concepts and have misinterpreted the law. It is my job to correct their erroneous way of thinking." "Master," rejoined R. Akiva, "the debate between you and all the other sages has persisted so long without resolution that it has generated considerable anger and frustration. A number of us fear that this partisan zealotry will split the Academy and result in harm to you, the Academy and possibly the whole Jewish community. It is not unusual for the sages to hold differing views, and then the matter is decided in favor of the opinion of the majority. Why not follow that principle?" The older man slowly shook his head back and forth, "No, the truth must be sought, and when found, followed. It is my duty to convince the others of the error of their thinking." When they reached the Academy, Rabbi Eliezer went directly in to take his appointed place, while his disciple turned to join several colleagues standing near the entrance.

From this encounter we can see that R. Akiva agreed with the position of his teacher, but still advised R. Eliezer to ignore the truth and take the side of the majority to please the sages. He sacrificed principles to consensus "Why not follow the majority?" In refusing this course, R. Eliezer sought to persuade the members of the Sanhedrin of the correctness of his opinion using a brilliant analysis of relevant Halakha. Before resorting to miracles, R. Eliezer first presented all the arguments in the world. When this route proved ineffectual, he sought to justify his position through a series of miraculous deeds—tearing a carob-tree from its roots and placing it some one hundred cubits away; reversing the direction of a stream of water; and forcing the walls of a building bent until it nearly fell. None of these miracles altered the Sages' perspective. They remained unwavering in their objection to R. Eliezer's point of view. Having witnessed their inexorability, R. Eliezer exclaimed in desperation, "If the Law agrees with me, let it be proven from Heaven!" Whereupon a voice from heaven cried out: "Why do you dispute with Rabbi Eliezer, seeing that in all matters the Law agrees with him!"

In the Talmudic tradition, there are many stories of heavenly voices that were treated with awe and respect as the divine voices of God revealing judgment to men. Since the prophecy ceased, a heavenly divine voice remained the sole means of communication between God and man. Throughout the history of the Bible, God's heavenly voice has spoken to Adam, Abraham, Moses, the prophets, and any other man, great or small, to whom God decided pronounce His judgment. Thus, we come across the story of R Eleazar from Modiin whom Bar Kokhba killed, when a heavenly voice pronounced the judgment against him: "Woe to the worthless shepherd who abandons his flock! Let a sword descend upon his arm and his right eye. His arm will wither and his right eye will be blinded" (Jerusalem Talmud Ta'anit (4:6, 68d-69a; Zech. 11:17).

In another instance, at the point when R. Akiva's life expired at the hands of the cruel Roman executioners, a *bath kol* called out, declaring that his soul deserved eternal life in the World-to-Come. "It is not in Heaven," boldly answered the rabbis. "The Torah has already been revealed at Mount Sinai. We, therefore, need not be concerned with further Heavenly Voices" (Deuteronomy 30: 12). This is very arrogant and challenging answer. That the Torah is 'not in heaven' or 'beyond the sea' does not have to be literally understood that the Torah may have been found in such faraway places. These verses metaphorically express that the laws of the Torah not too high or not too deep or far away for people to learn and obey them. The rabbis insisted that God gave them the right to judge the matters of law according to the majority rule, as the analysis of the Deuteronomy verses attests: "And you shall come to the priests the Levites, and to the judge that shall be in those days, and inquire; and they shall show you the sentence of judgment" (17:9). Moreover, it says that the sentence of the law that they shall be judged on should be followed without hesitation neither 'to the right hand, nor to the left' (17:11). The rabbis also referred to the instruction in Exodus to "Follow the majority's ruling" (23:2) as 'proof' that majority rule is the will of God. This verse is the bulwark that they use to ward off any logical criticism of the principle. Hence, their bold statement that, 'We do not need obey voices from Heaven.'

It may be that some of the sages recognized the correctness of R. Eliezer's interpretation, but did not want to break with their peers. R. Eliezer, however, insisted on following his own principles rather than merely cowing to popular opinion, thus heeding Scriptural commands: "You shall not follow a crowd to do evil; nor shall you testify in a dispute so as to turn aside after many to pervert justice"; and "Thou shalt not follow the many to evil; neither shalt thou bear witness in a cause so as to incline after the many to pervert judgment" (Exodus 23:2). However, this Scriptural verse is taken out of context by the proponents of the majority rule and testifies against them, particularly as it applies to the events of the R. Eliezer's trial. It is not disputable whether God allowed the rabbis to judge by majority rule. It is a Scriptural fact. The question is how and when to apply this commandment. The Torah explicitly teaches that "You shall not follow a crowd to do evil; nor shall you testify in a dispute so as to turn aside after many to pervert justice," and "Keep you far from a false matter," as "I will not justify the wicked." These are the principles of God's majority rule as expressed in the Torah. Were these principles upheld by the sages of the Sanhedrin in the trial of R. Eliezer? Not at all. In this shameful trial justice was perverted and did not serve the purpose of God's Torah. R. Eliezar was not only treated disrespectfully, but grossly abused, humiliated, and excommunicated. Can the majority be wrong? Sure they can. That is why God says that one should neither follow the many to evil nor testify in dispute to accommodate the majority in preventing justice. In their decisions, the majority should follow the goodness of the holy Torah, not earthy authorities, politics, and personal ambitions. The strength of the majority is not in numbers, but in finding and upholding the truth of the Torah by reflecting God's justice and love. Democracy by majority rule is a noble pursuit, but Judaism is not democracy but the fulfillment of the will of God on earth, which has been upheld by only few. As R. Yisrael Rutman says, "In Judaism, power does not derive from the people, but from God. The majority rules, insofar as it does, because God say so, not because majority say so." Certainly, the will of God was not reflected in the outcome of R. Eliezer's trial.

R. Eliezer showed that the Aknai oven was Levitically pure, and a Heavenly voice immediately approved the veracity of his case. The sages did not question the truthfulness and authenticity of the *Bath-Kol*. There were no doubt in the minds of the sages of the Sanhedrin that R. Eliezer's *Halakhah* was right and, that there was therefore no need for the majority rule to decide the strictly legal issue because the case was clearly established in support of R. Eliezer's view. For the sages to say, 'We do not obey voices from Heaven' sounds like rejection of God Himself. In their wrongdoing the sages blamed God for defending R. Eliezer and even used God's words, albeit out of context (Deuteronomy 23:2), against Him. By their actions they tried to force the Lawgiver to stay out of the courts and not interfere with the legal authority of the rabbis to exercise their duties. Even if the Torah was given to the Israelites on Mount Sinai a long time ago and the God of Israel allowed the rabbis to decide legal and everyday affairs by the principle of majority rule, it does not mean that the Almighty suddenly disappeared, vanished from human sight, and no longer interfered in their daily politico-religious and spiritual lives. None the great men of the Bible—David, Solomon, and the prophets— excluded God from their lives; on the contrary, they lived by every word issued by the living God.

Later on, to justify their decision in the trial in the eyes of others, they came up with the strange Talmudic story that God was pleased and approved their actions. According to the story, the Palestinian Tanna of the third generation (second century), R. Nathan, met the prophet Elijah and asked him what God thought of the outcome of the Aknai oven trial. Elijah answered that God laughed and replied, "My sons have defeated Me, My sons have defeated Me" (Babylonian Talmud, Baba Metzia 59b). By the way, the same R. Nathan who was a high Talmudic authority, together with R. Meir (the closest student of R. Akiva), at one time conspired to depose R. Simon from the Presidency of the Sanhedrin and usurp his authority themselves; but the plot came to Rabban knowledge, and he caused the conspirators to be expelled from the school (Baba Bathra 131a). It was not the first time that R. Nathan had taken part in the politico-religious plot, this time to accommodate majority rule for the Sanhedrin's authorities and eradicate any dissent in rabbinical affairs. The fictitiousness of this fantastic story reminds us of a few stories that we retold in the previous chapters: how R. Akiva married the wife of the Roman Governor of Judea Rufus, or how the rabbis executed Bar Kokhba for being the wrong messiah. What makes these legends synonymous is the fact that they contain not a drop of the truth and have to be treated as anecdotes, not as historical facts. For God, who defended R. Eliezer on this trial and perfectly knew the righteousness of his position, to admit that, as the story implies, the sages in their wrong and corrupted decision 'defeated and bested Me' is a blasphemy and insult. How could the sages have defeated and bested God, if He by the very nature of His Holy essence of goodness, righteousness, and love stands against injustice and wrongdoing?

The main concern of the sages was not the Halachic controversy on the subject of the ritual purity (or impurity) of the Aknai oven but the inflexible will of R. Eliezer. Chosen as a scapegoat and singled out as an example for others who might have dared to rebel against the rule of the majority, his trial served as the ultimate reminder that dissent would not be tolerated. In the political-religious environment following the destruction of the Second Temple, and in the context of Roman subjugation, the sages recognized that the survival of Judaism depended upon a centralized religious authority to extinguish individual dissent. What makes R. Eliezer's trial fundamentally significant, then, is that it served as a key moment in the majority rule among the Sages of the Sanhedrin. Individual opinions of rebellious scholars (*'zaken mamre'*) such as R. Eliezer would not be tolerated.

During his trail, not one sage said a word in R. Eliezer's defense, not even his closest disciple, Rabbi Akiva, who remained silent throughout. In her book *The Talmud Revisited: Tragedy and the Oven of Aknai*, Rabbi Janet Maden identifies the paradox at the heart of the matter. For in putting R. Eliezer on trial, what the sages demonstrated was their own spiritual impurity rather than that of the oven: "In ignoring the dicta that all Israel is responsible for one another, that one should not wrong his neighbor, and that one who causes *ona'at devarim* in public forfeits his share in the world-to-come, the Sages clearly indicate that they are not motivated merely by the desire to settle matters of *Halakha*. In intentionally and publicly inflicting *ona'at devarim* upon R. Eliezer, the Sages forfeit their claim to wisdom as surely as they display their own spiritual impurity; appropriately, the revelation of their spiritual nadir comes at the height of narrative tension." When R. Eliezer witnessed the sage's intransigence, he looked over the entire assembly for a long time, and then, with head erect, he turned and left the Sanhedrin.

Excommunication

As soon as R. Eliezer left the House of Study, the Sages pronounced all the parts of the 'snake-oven' unclean and burned them.

In the same afternoon the President of the Sanhedrin Rabban Gamaliel spoke to the Sages. "Rabotai," he said, "this morning

Rabbi Eliezer refused to go along with the wishes of the majority of the Sages. He had the audacity to challenge the authority of this Sanhedrin and appeal to Heaven. After you called out in response to the Heavenly Voice that the Torah is not in Heaven and that the Torah we have received instructs us to incline after the majority, the Voice was silent. And yet, Rabbi Eliezer persisted in insisting on his interpretation of the Law and left the Assembly. In so doing he has separated himself from our community. According to Jewish law, insisting on minority views overruled by the majority is a cause for imposing a ban or excommunication on the individual. Therefore I and the other leaders of the Assembly have concluded that a ban should be imposed on Rabbi Eliezer ben Hyrcanus. Such a ruling by this Assembly would mean that Rabbi Eliezer no longer could come to this House of Assembly and participate in our deliberations, and members of this Sanhedrin could not visit and study with him. This ruling is now placed before the Sanhedrin for a vote."

No voices were raised either in agreement or disagreement with this decision. Rabban Gamaliel looked sternly at Rabbi Joshua who had disagreed frequently with him in the past. Rabbi Joshua responded quietly, "I agree with the decision of our leaders." R. Joshua would not say otherwise. At one time he refused to conform, arguing with Rabban Gamaliel on many occasions. But his life became more complicated as a result, and the public humiliations and administrative pressure from the office of the Nasi turned unbearable. Presumably R. Joshua could not forget the harassment of Rabban Gamaliel, who had ordered him to stay in front of all the Assembly while the Nasi was sitting and speaking to the sages. Many times R. Joshua had retracted his arguments and been compelled to assent to the heavy hand of the patriarch (Babylonian Talmud, Berakhot 27b-28a).

Then Rabbi Gamaliel looked at Rabbi Akiva, a disciple of Rabbi Eliezer. But strangely, Rabbi Akiva said nothing. The most prominent disciple of R. Eliezer would not say a word in defense of his beloved teacher and highly respected master. By this time, R. Akiva's importance and influence were well established among the aristocratic rabbinical hierarchy and academic scholars; he had become a recognized spiritual and religious leader of the nation. He would later demonstrate his ability to influence and mobilize the majority of the rabbis, including the Sages of the Academy and Sanhedrin, in full support of Bar Kokhba and his Revolt. Even an authority figure like Rabban Gamaliel considered it an honor and duty to ask R. Akiva's opinion. Convinced of the necessity of a central authority for Judaism, R. Akiva became a devoted adherent and friend of Gamaliel, and aspired one day to become himself the patriarch and true spiritual chief of the Jews (Rosh Hashanah ii. 9). Rabban Gamaliel did not insist on the vote of R. Akiva; it was deemed unnecessary as the decision to ban R. Eliezer had already been made with R. Akiva's approval.

Did R. Akiva not sense a *"Chillul HaShem"* in the making? Did he not realize that the excommunication of R. Eliezer constituted the public humiliation of a great scholar, as well as an extraordinary act of disrespect for his teacher and desecration of the name of God? In other words, did he not know that the actions of the Sages were equivalent to bringing dishonor and shame to God's name? As the Talmud reminds us, "Whoever shames another in public is like one who sheds blood," and "He who publicly puts his neighbor to shame has no portion in the world-to-come" (Babylonian Talmud, Bava Metzia 58b). Even his own disciple, the great Rashbi, commented that is better for man jump into the firing furnace, rather than shame his fellow man in public. Surely R. Akiva was aware of the implications of their decision, but for the reasons we will come to, remained silent.

A vote was taken and the decision of the leadership was approved unanimously. What is noteworthy here is the fact that the excommunication of R. Eliezer was decided upon in his absence. He was not given a chance to defend himself against the accusations.

"Both Opinions are the Words of the Living God"

What was R. Eliezer's so-called crime? He merely defended his position against the majority of the sages, confident of its correctness. Maintaining a minority opinion does not constitute a crime. But without a doubt, the opinions of the sages in the court of law threatened as 'the living word of God'. Certainly, R. Eliezer did not deserve the cruel and unjustified treatment of the sages or such harsh punishment for his dissent. A sage who disputes the opinion of his fellows—even after the Sanhedrin has ruled against his opinion—may continue to adhere to his opinion, so long as he does not rule accordingly for others. Such a sage will not be considered a "rebellious elder" (Mishnah, Sanhedrin 11:2). The Patriarch Abraham whom the Bible was called 'Ha-Ivri,' meaning the one from another side, heroically stood his ground against the majority of the pagan world. As today's reality testifies, his lonely (minority) beliefs has prevailed. Contemporary Judaism is the true manifestation of minority victory over majority rule.

In the past, when the sages were deciding on which opinion between Hillel and Shammai was correct, they ruled "that both opinions are the words of the living God, but the Law is in accordance with the School of Hillel" (Jerusalem Talmud, Berakoth 1d).

The Talmud says that in the time of the reduction of the Mishnah, there were the divergent views and disputes among the sages that were preserved and recorded. The Mishnah gives the reason for this practice: should a later court of law see fit to rule in accordance with minority opinion, it would be at liberty to do so. As Rabbi Judah says: "Why is the minority view recorded [in the

Mishnah] alongside the majority view? So that a [later] court that agrees with the minority view can rely on it" (Tosefta, Eduyyot 1:4). Rabbi Samson ben Abraham of Sens (French tosafist, c.1150-c.1230CE) understood the issue this way: "Even though the individual opinion was not accepted in the first instance, and the majority disagreed with the individual, a later generation may arise, the majority of whom might agree to the opinion of the individual, and then the matter will be decided in accordance with their opinion. All of the Torah was transmitted to Moses in this fashion: there are considerations to purify and considerations to render impure. [Moses] was told: How long will we have to clarify every situation? He said to them: "The rule is according to the majority (Berakoth 9a); however, *both opinions are the words of the living God*" (emphasis added).

This message of the Talmud teaches that even rejected opinions are potentially valuable Halakhic options in a future Ben Din under different circumstances. The beauty and the glory of the Torah lies in its diversity of the opinions, with each opinion having importance and contributing to the full spectrum of discussed Halakhah. Such is the way of the Holy Torah, for majority and minority opinions are both the words of the living God!

"Who will go and tell him?"

The story of R. Eliezer's trial and punishment is not yet over. Following the verdict of the sages, Rabban Gamaliel asked the sages, "Who will go and tell him?" Only then did Rabbi Akiva speak. "I will go and tell him, lest an unsuitable person go and tell him and thus destroy the whole world [that is, commit a great wrong by informing him tactlessly]." Of the subtext of Akiva's choice of words, Jeffrey L. Rubenstein says, "That the sages' actions are unjust become clear from Akiba's fear that if a man 'who is not fitting' informs Eliezer then the entire world will be destroyed. This shocking statement suggests that an outrage of tremendous proportions has been committed. Like the sin of the generation of the flood, the sages' offence threatens the existence of the world. Indeed, Eliezer's reaction to the ban confirms the fact that the sages have overreacted. His eyes 'streaming with tears' express anguish and suffering, not defiance and contempt."

It was not the first time that R. Akiva had spuriously volunteered "trying to help" R. Eliezer. Once R. Eliezer was arrested for heresy, tried by a Roman judge, and almost immediately released (by mistake). Not able to recall the cause of the accusation and feeling profoundly distressed, R. Eliezer asked his student if he remember anything improper in his past. R. Akiva "helped" his master to recollect long past events, and eventually succeeded in comforting him (Babylonian Talmud, Abodah Zarah 165, 17a, and the Tosefta, Hullin 2.24). Why would R. Akiva suddenly break his silence and volunteer to bring R. Eliezer the news of his excommunication? If he felt sorry for his former teacher and wanted to spare him having the news reach him by a formal source, why did he not move to defend him during the trial and sentencing? For R. Akiva to stay silent during the trial only to tell his master of his cruel sentence afterwards must have merely deepened R. Eliezer's sense of betrayal. The damage of complicity had already been done, and there was no recompense in this insignificant, singular act. Besides, the Talmud reveals that R. Eliezer had already known of his punishment because R. Akiva was not the first man who brought him the difficult news: "When Yose son of Damascene visited R. Eliezer in Lydda and brought him news of the vote taken in the academy, whereupon Eliezer burst in tears and said: "Go tell them, do not worry about your voting! I received the identical teaching from Rabban Yohanan ben Zakkai who received it from his teacher who in turn received it from his teacher, a Halakha transmitted to Moses from Sinai"

(Midrash Yadayim 4:3; Tosefta Yadayim 2:16). So what was the R. Akiva's intention by agreeing to go personally to R. Eliezer to relay the verdict? Was it out of love and compassion—a desire to safeguard his master from the harshness of hearing the official sentence of the Sanhedrin from a less familiar source? Was it to spare his teacher that "he donned black garments and wrapped himself in black" as a sign of mourning and demonstration of compassion?

R. Eliezer was astonished to see disciple dressed in mourning attire. "Akiva," he asked, "what has particularly happened today?" "Master," he replied with sadness, "it appears to me that thy companions hold aloof from you." By answering this way, R. Akiva tried to convince his master that he had nothing to do with the decision of the sages. If he really loved his master so much, why would he ceremoniously separate himself at a distance of four cubits from him, instead of hugging and kissing him? What prevented him from displaying feelings of love and kindness to his mortally ill master? Was it ever-present yearning aspiration to 'bite the sage in a manner of donkey'? One thing is certain, and that is the despair of R. Eliezer, whom we read, "Thereupon R. Eliezer rent his garments, put off his shoes, and sat on the earth, whilst tears streamed from his eyes. The world was then smitten: a third of the olive crop, a third of the wheat, and a third of the barley crop" (Babylonian Talmud: Tractate Baba Mezi'a 59b). Another tradition says, "Great was that day, for everything at which R. Eliezer looked was burned up."

The Snake-Like Aknai Oven

Perhaps the reason for R. Akiva's offer lies in the fact that he was covertly involved in the shameful trial and satisfied with its results. As an experienced politician and diplomat, he skillfully planned his role in the affair of the Aknai oven, all the time remaining unnoticed in the background. The persona of the snake in the Book of Genesis (3:1), with its sinister cleverness and quiet deviousness, readily comes to mind. It is not without reason that the Talmud compares the mighty rhetorical arguments that the sages deployed against R. Eliezer to the segments of a snake-oven. As Rab Judah said in Samuel's name: "It means that they encompassed it with arguments as a snake, and proved it unclean" (Baba Mezi'a 59b).

Drawing on the symbolic resonances with the metaphor of the snake, Jeffrey L. Rubenstein writes: "The sages ruled the segmented oven impure by surrounding R. Eliezer with 'words like this snake' (snake-oven). This expression simply connotes the meaning that the sages spoke with cunning and guile. These words ring of personal assault. A snake surrounds its pray by squeezing, choking, and suffocating it to death. Eliezer was treated in a cruel and unkind fashion. While God tolerates—even approves—his sons defeating the 'father', He will not permit his sons to wrong one another. 'All the gates are locked except for the gates of wronging'" (Psalms 39:13).

Thanks to the quiet diplomacy of R. Akiva and his very influential closest cycle of plotters, the sages were determined to punish R. Eliezer. That this trial and its sentence were predetermined and had strong overtones of a political power game among the sages has been noticed by many theologians. Joseph Ehrlich describes the trial as "a political power play and coup where evil intertwined itself gaining political, academic and religious control." Elie Wiezel, a survivor of the Auschwitz and Buchenwald concentration camps, and the author of 57 books, and a recipient of the Nobel Peace Prize and Presidential Medal of Freedom, says: "When Rabbi Eliezer the Great, a revered sage, saw corruption and evil in the Sanhedrin, the Jewish court, he single-handedly staged a protest and was excommunicated." Rabbi

Arthur Segal contests the tactics of manipulation and deviousness deployed by Eliezer's contemporaries: "Politics are also in play with the redaction of the life story and excommunication of Rabbi Eliezer ben Hyrcanus."

This trial revealed that a new era had begun. The highest court of the land, Sanhedrin, made its ruling only by the majority, and refused to tolerate—and indeed persecuted—any individual dissent. Even the intervention of God, in whatever form (heavenly voice, sign or miracle) would not change the sages' majority decision. R. Eliezer was the last sage who stood his ground against taking the God of Israel away from His central role in the everyday Jewish people affairs, and against injustice and abuse of power by the President and the sages of the Sanhedrin. Tragically his lonely voice was neglected and ultimately stamped out, so that evil and corruption prevailed.

The Relationship between the Master and the Student

To remove R. Eliezer from his position of prominence and fame and establish majority rule—thus superseding his conservative approach to the interpretation of Jewish laws, tradition, and prophecy, and so clear the way for a new generation of his followers with himself as its rising star—was a long cherished dream of R. Akiva's. To borrow his own metaphor, one might say that he wished to bite his former teacher so badly that he might never recover. He had long nursed grievances and resentments towards R. Eliezer and other members of the Academy, and this, together with old sage's stubbornness and inexorable will of iron, did not bode well for his future relationship with his master and mentor. From the start, this relationship with his master was pathologically uncivil. As a young scholar of sensitive temperament, R. Akiva endured the humiliation of teasing and mockery about his age, ancestry, illiteracy, and ignorance.

Never known for his sensitivity or affableness, R. Eliezer was extremely stubborn and domineering with the students; he did not tolerate disagreements, feverishly upheld the old traditions and teachings of his Masters, and was "a bitter controversialist from his youth until death" (Weiss, Doroth II, 82). However, other sources say that R. Eliezer was not seeking quarrels; that the *oven-snake* trial was the only instance recorded in the Talmud, when he defended his views against the majority, and that he was a peaceful and humble man (Halevi, Doroth 1, 5).

During the first thirteen years that R. Akiva spent in the house of study, his teachers, R. Eliezer and R. Joshua, paid little attention or largely ignored him. This constant humiliation and rejection embittered his attitude towards the learned Torah community to the extent that, as we know, he dreamed of revenge by "biting them [his teachers and fellow scholars] as so badly to crush their bones in a manner of donkey." Adding more fuel to the fire was that the old elite among the sages thoroughly denounced his inclusion as a member of the Sanhedrin. Perhaps such rejection is what led R. Akiva to aspire to become not only the spiritual leader and the teacher of Israel, but also the *Nasi*, the President of Sanhedrin, and the political leader of the nation. The lack of pedigree—the fact that he was from a converted family—prevented him from achieving his goal. *Akiva ben Yosef haGer* (i.e. convert) was not considered a suitable candidate for the President of the Sanhedrin.

Rabbi Tarfon was also not a member of the Sanhedrin as he suffered the same lack of pedigree as R. Akiva. He used to say on behalf of R. Akiva and himself, "Were we members of the Sanhedrin, no person would ever be put to death." Thereupon Rabban Simeon ben Gamaliel, the Nasi of the Sanhedrin, remarked: "If so these rabbis would multiply shedders of blood in Israel" (Tractate Makkot 7a).

R. Akiva suspected that his teacher played a part in the Sanhedrin affair against him, revenging him for his numerous public challenges in the matters of Halakha, Aggadah, and prophecy. He was familiar with R. Eliezer's sayings regarding converted Jews. According to teachings, R. Eliezer would say "Why did the Torah warn against [the wronging of] a proselyte in thirty-six, or as others says, in forty-six, places? Because he has a strong inclination to evil" (Baba Metzia 59b). Rashi explained this remark as follows: "Original character of the proselyte is bad, and evil treatment might cause him to relapse" (Horayoth 13a). Indeed, his teacher perceived many of R. Akiva's secret fears and resentments, which he had carried in his heart since the initial years of his studies in the Academy.

Some authors have described the controversies between these giants of the Torah as the collision of the two sides, where the 'left side' represents old tradition and strict justice that knows only the truth of the Law. (Whether or not others accept this truth is irrelevant, which is why R. Eliezer could not accept the majority vote). The 'right side' represents the concept of divine mercy, forgiveness and kindness embodied by R. Akiva. To put it simply, the two sides reflect the controversies that persisted between the houses of Shammai and Hillel. R. Eliezer was excommunicated because he was 'Shamuti' from the house of Shammai.

The other explanations of the conflict between these renowned scholars speak of the two worlds: one is before the destruction of the Second Temple, represented by R. Eliezer and generations of his teachers; the other one is after destruction of the Temple, represented by R. Akiva and the young generation of his followers.

CHAPTER VIII

The Death of R. Eliezer

An Unexpected Visit

Now we are approaching the finale of this dramatic story. After the imposition of the ban, R Eliezer lived in retirement with his wife, Ima Shalom. He was well removed from the center of Torah learning, though occasionally some of his disciples visited him and informed of the transactions of the Sanhedrin (Yadayim 4:3). It was during this difficult time of rejection and humiliation that R. Eliezer said: "Let the honor of thy colleague be as dear to thee as thine own, and be not easily moved to anger. Repent one day before thy death. Warm thyself by the fire of the wise men, but be cautious of their burning coals ['slight them not'] that thou be not burned; for their bite is the bite of a jackal, their sting is that of a scorpion, their hissing is that of a snake, and all their words are fiery coals (reflection on Ecclesiastes 9:8; Talmud, Shabbat 153a). Repent one day before dying!" When the disciples inquired as to how it was possible to know on which day they would die, he replied: "That is just what I mean. Because a person does not know when he will die, he must therefore repent every day!"

When R. Eliezer fell fatally sick, R. Akiva and his companions went to visit him. That day was the Sabbath eve. The sages, seeing that R. Eliezer's mind was clear, entered his chamber and sat down at a distance of four cubits. "Why have you come?" he asked them. "To study the Torah," they replied. "And why did you not come before now?" he asked. They answered, "We had no time."

This very short Talmudic story raises serious questions. As the story goes, R. Eliezer had been sick for a while, maybe for a few days or weeks. The Talmud does not specify the length of his sickness, but it also does not say that R. Eliezer suddenly became sick on the Friday afternoon that happened to be the last day of his life. The explanation for Rabbis' unexpected visit may lie with Ima Shalom, his wife. Perhaps she understood that her husband would not live much longer and was about to expire, so she expeditiously notified them. It is clear that R. Akiva and his companions were visiting the excommunicated R. Eliezer for the first time ("And why did you not come before now?"). He had been banned as the result of the famous dispute regarding the Aknai oven, and as the story relates, it was also the last time they would see him alive.

The Duty to Visit the Sick

Something is grossly wrong here. Why did the sages not travel to see their sick colleague before his dying day? While the rules did not allow the members of the Sanhedrin to visit an excommunicated person, what about his most renowned disciple, R. Akiva, with his inner cycle of very influential rabbis who were not members of the Sanhedrin? R. Akiva would become the spiritual leader of the nation, the "Father of all Sages," and yet did not come to see his sick beloved master!

Recall the story recorded in the Babylonian Talmud of one of R. Akiva's students falling ill and none of the sages visiting him except for R. Akiva (Nedarim 40a). Because of this tremendous honor, the student recovered and said, "Rebbe, you have brought me life". Afterwards, R. Akiva gathered his students and lectured them, "Anyone who does not visit the sick is as if he has spilled blood." Rav Dimi went further to declare that, "Anyone who visits the sick causes him to live and anyone who does not visit the sick causes him to die" (ibid.).

There is another wonderful story in the Talmud entitled *Beauty*. It illuminates the love and care of the rabbis according to the commandments of the Torah, especially to those who become helpless and sick: "Rabbi Elaezar fell ill, and Rabbi Jochanan went to visit him. Rabbi Eleazar was lying in a dark room, but Rabbi Jochanan bared his arm, and such was the beauty of Rabbi Jochanan that the room became full of light. So they sat down and wept together" (Talmud: Berakhot 5b). What was wrong with R. Akiva? He raged against those who failed to visit sick comrades and compared them to killers, yet did not honor his sick teacher, whom he had acknowledged to the word as his "master." Such hypocrisy reveals the kind of relationship that existed between R. Akiva and R. Eliezer. Despite our knowledge of R. Akiva's character, we still wonder why 24,000 of his disciples had so many imperfections, suffered tragic flaws, were condemned by Heavenly court, and died a horrible death. It is easier to blame the students for their fate, as the majority of the authors have, than to attribute the real cause of their downfall to their spiritual teacher and leader.

"I will be surprised if these die a natural death"

R. Eliezer was well aware of his student's lack of love and honor for his master, and that knowledge caused him excruciating pain. When he saw R. Akiva in the last moments before he died, he still hoped that his celebrated disciple would throw himself in his arms and that they would weep in joy and forgive each other. Instead, R. Akiva ceremoniously sat down at the distance of four cubits from his banned teacher and to his Master's question of "Why did you come?" answered, "To learn Torah from you!" Such an arrogant answer from the disciple who suddenly decided to learn the Torah from his dying teacher at his deathbed begs the question of why he could not find time for study when R. Eliezer was well. One would think that visiting one's sick master would take precedence among a student's duties and obligations.

That was exactly the point that was underscoring when he asked the sages the reason for their not coming before. R. Akiva and his companions unsympathetically answered that they lacked the time. Their insensible attitude must have filled the dying master with indignation. He realized that his hope of forgiveness of, and reconciliation with, the sages—and especially with R. Akiva—had faded away. He then pointed a hand at the sages and said, "I will be surprised if these die a natural death." Immediately, R. Akiva recollected the story of his student Yehudah ben Nehemiah, who disrespected R. Tarfon in a dispute between them and to whom R. Akiva said almost the same words, "I wonder whether you will live long." As his disciple R. Yehudah ben Ila'i testified that Yehudah ben Nehemiah had passed away shortly after this encounter (Menachot 68b).

"And what will my death be?" R. Akiva cautiously asked with a trembling voice. R. Eliezer fastened his gaze on R. Akiva's eyes for a long time and slowly but distinctly delivered the sentence, "Yours will be more cruel than theirs." R. Eliezer knew of R. Akiva's wrongdoing towards him. The God of Israel had revealed to him the future of R. Akiva and this particular group of sages. Fifteen years after R. Eliezer's pronouncement, all of them would die at the hands of Roman executioners as the participants in the Bar Kokhba Revolt. They would die exactly in the manner that R. Eliezer had predicted. The whole of this dialogue is recorded in the Babylonian Talmud (Tractate Sanhedrin, folio 68a).

The Divine Gates of Tears are Always Open

The tears of a person who has been publicly humiliated go directly to heaven and divine retribution follows. R. Eleazar said, "Since the destruction of the Temple, the gates of prayer are locked, for it is written, 'Also when I cry out, He shutteth out my prayer'" (Lamentations 3:8). Yet though the gates of prayer are locked, the gates of tears are not, for it is written, "Hear my prayer, O Lord, and give ear unto my cry; hold not thy peace at my tears" (Psalms 34:13). God always hears and responds to the cry of the victim of verbal abusing, slander, and defamation. Take the example of the death of the President of the Sanhedrin, Rabban Gamaliel, under whose corrupted authority R. Eliezer was unjustly banned. As he used to say, "Whoever has mercy on other people, Heaven will have mercy upon him; whoever does not have mercy on other people, Heaven will not have mercy upon him" (Sabb. 151b). His own words testified against him.

That same Friday evening, while engrossed in the study of the holy Torah with his students and sages, and answering *"tahor"* (pure) on the final question, R. Eliezer's saintly soul departed for heaven. Immediately after hearing and witnessing this, R. Joshua arose and exclaimed, "The vow is annulled, the vow is annulled!" (Babylonian Talmud, Tractate Sanhedrin, 68a).

Despite having been excommunicated, R. Eliezer is quoted in the Mishnah, the Baraita, and the Talmud more frequently than any of his colleagues, with more than 300 halachot (laws) recorded in Mishnah and an equal number in the Tosefta and the Baraitot. He is also the putative author of a work known as *The Ethics of Rabbi Eliezer.*

From Rejection to Blessing

At the conclusion of the Sabbath the remains of R. Eliezer were carried from Caesarea to Lydda, where he had formerly conducted his academy, and there he was buried. In his eulogy R. Joshua reportedly kissed the stone on which R. Eliezer used to sit while instructing his pupils, and said, "This stone represents Sinai [where the Law was revealed]; and he who sat on it represented the Ark of the Covenant" (Canticles Rabbah 1:3). From another Talmudic source we learn that R. Joshua stood by the deathbed of Eliezer b. Hyrcanus and called to him: "O Master, thou art of more value to Israel than God's gift of the rain; since the rain gives life in this world only, whereas thou givest life both in this world and in the world to come" (Babylonian Talmud: Tractate Sanhedrin, folio 101a).

Curiously, the very same people who publicly humiliated and disgraced R. Eliezer during his trial suddenly admired and praised him once he fell deathly ill. According to rabbinical sources, when R. Eliezer fell sick, four elders went to visit him: R. Tarfon, R. Joshua, R. Eleazar b. Azariah, and R. Akiba. At that time, R. Tarfon commended him in the highest terms: "Thou art more valuable to Israel than rain; for rain is [precious] in this world, whereas thou art [so] for this world and the next." By this he meant that as a result of R. Eliezer's teachings Israel would enjoy a reward in the next life. R. Joshua praised him in a similarly effusive manner: "Thou art more valuable to Israel than the sun's disc: the sun's disc is but for this world, whilst my master is for this world and the next." This comment was then followed by R. Eleazar b. Azariah's observation that, "Thou art better to Israel than a father and a mother: these are for this world, whereas my master is for this world and the next" (Ibid.).

In extolling the virtues of R. Eliezer, the sages gave the impression that they were competing with each other for the best eulogy, trying to justify their previous behavior in the eyes of the heavenly court. If they had treated and respected R. Eliezer in terms consistent with their praise, the great sage would not have been humiliated, and a great tragedy of excommunication could have been avoided.

Repentance and Reconciliation

What was R. Akiva's reaction to the death of his master? R. Eliezer's self-referential comment that "There is a fierce wrath in the world" (Babylonian Talmud: Tractate Sanhedrin Folio 101a) suggested that God was angry with him, hence his suffering. At this, the disciples broke into tears, but R. Akiva laughed. "Why are you laughing?" they asked him, "Why do you weep?" he retorted. "Shall the Scroll of the Torah lie in pain, and we not weep?" He replied, "For that very reason I rejoice." While the scholars stood with their teacher on his deathbed, R. Akiva explained, "You see, my Master was prosperous and completely successful in everything. He enjoyed an ideal life. I had a suspicion, God forbid, that he may have received all his rewards in this world, living nothing for the next world to come; but now that I see him lying in pain and suffering, I rejoice, knowing that he has been purged of whatever minute sin he may have committed, and his reward has been treasured up for him in the next world."

R. Eliezer said to him, "Akiba, have I neglected anything of the whole Torah?" By this he meant to ask if R. Akiva was implying that his master was suffering in the present for his sins, so that he may have nothing but reward in the world-to-come. R. Akiva replied, "Thou, O Master, has taught us, for there is not a just man upon earth, that does good and sin not. Suffering is precious" (Ecclesiast 7:20; Babylonian Talmud, Tractate Sanhedrin 101a). "Akiva, you have comforted me. Akiva, you have comforted me," wearily whispered R. Eliezer with a scarcely perceptible and a cunning smile.

When the Sabbath was finished, R. Akiba met the bier of R. Eliezer as it was carried from Caesarea to Lydda. As lightning pierced the dark sky, R. Akiva suddenly grasped the significance of his master's death. The pain of loss was finally real. For R. Akiva, the death deprived him of a father figure, a wise teacher, and a righteous friend. He tormented himself and could not forgive his disgraceful behavior towards his master. In his grief R. Akiva beat his head until blood flowed. This time it was not the pretend grief and feigned tears that he simulated on the night of his teacher's death. In a furious fit of self-loathing and self-flagellation, he found no reprieve from the pain. His tears and blood mixed together and trickled down, as his lips feverishly whispered a prayer of repentance. With heartfelt remorse, he pleaded with his master and God to forgive him.

Unexpectedly, he heard R. Eliezer's voice: "Akiva, my son, with the great gratitude I am accepting your repentance. My soul is exulting in happiness. I am forgiving you too and begging your forgiveness for my sins against you." Astonished, R. Akiva hardly pronounced: "Master, your voice . . . It is so familiar and at the same time . . . It sounds strange, different . . . I never heard you speak like this . . . Please do not perform your magic tricks on me. I well remember the carrot tree and stream of water in the House of Study, and how you planted a whole field of cucumbers by merely saying a magic word . . . Is it really you, my beloved master? God knows how thankful and happy I am that you are talking to me and forgive my treacherous behavior . . . You took a heavy burden from my shoulders, and my soul is bursting with joy . . . O, my Master, only now do I realize what wrong I have done you . . . My greatest wish is to embrace you, hold you in my arms, and weep with you . . . If you only knew how I wish to show you my grief and my love . . ." Red tears of gratitude unceasingly rolled from his eyes.

Then the voice of R. Eliezer sounded more sonorous and distinct: "Akiva, my son, have no doubts, it is me, your Master. There is something I have to tell you. On Saturday eve you opened my eyes when you were laughing while I was suffering before death. Do you remember, how you said that 'Suffering is precious?' God indeed punished me for my sins in this life. Now, since He cleansed me, I can testify that your words are true, for I received my reward in another world. I was worrying a great deal about you. When you became the *Father of the Sages* and achieved prominence among the scholars of the Torah, your life was fulfilled with success and happiness. You have a loving and wise wife in Rachel, whom you adorned with the crown of 'a Jerusalem of gold'. You eat, dress, and sleep surrounded by gold and silver. When your students saw Rachel go out wearing sandals of gold and a *city of gold* upon her head, they said to you, 'Our teacher, you embarrassed us.'" You answered them, "She suffered much with me in the study of the Torah" (Avot DeRabi Nathan Ver. 1:6). "You also have good and learned children and enormous wealth," continued voice of R. Eliezer. "Forgive me, but I thought that, God forbid, you had received all your rewards in this world and would not merit life in the World-to-Come. You remember what kind of death I predicted for you? When God revealed it to me on that Friday night, my heart was rejoicing for you. I could not burst out laughing due to my physical pain and weakness, but my soul was full of happiness for you. Akiva, my son, great and staggering events will shake and rock the Judea and the Roman world to their foundation, and you will be directly involved in them. For all your sins God will commit you to the hands of the cruel executioners. Do not give way to despair. God also will give you the strength and courage to face the agony of your death. This punishment will open for you the gate of the World-to-Come, and your reward will be guaranteed. As you have said, 'Everything God does is to the best.' Also, do not worry any more about your coins. There is a money changer in my World, the Almighty God of Israel. Only here the Divine Torah can be completely and perfectly learned and understood. We will laugh together about how limited and distorted our knowledge of the Torah was. Much Torah have I learned, yet I have but skimmed from the knowledge of my teachers as much as a dog lapping from the sea. Much Torah have I taught, yet my disciples have only drawn from me as much as a painting stick from its tube . . . Be patient, my son, when the appointed time arrives and you come up hither, your soul will rejoice in the presence of the saints and in the glory of God who you will see face to face . . ."

Rabbi Akiva, excessively agitated and trembling, but overflowing with joy and thankfulness to his Master, solemnly pronounced, "My father, my father, the chariot of Israel and the horsemen thereof" (2 Kings 2:12; Babylonian Talmud, Sanhedrin 68a).

CHAPTER IX

The Ten Lost Tribes of Israel Will Return

"For, Lo, I will command and I will sift the House of Israel among all nations like as corn is sifted in a sieve, yet shall not the least grain fall upon the earth" (Amos 9:9).

The Biblical History of the Ten Tribes

Before proceeding any further, let us clarify the difference between the nations called the 'House of Judah' and the 'House of Israel' (the Ten Tribes). The divine Torah was revealed to Moses circa 1313BCE at Mount Sinai. The People whom Moses led out of Egypt called themselves Israelites or Hebrews: Abram the Hebrew (Genesis 14:3), Joseph the Hebrew (Genesis 39:14), God of the Hebrews (Exodus 5:3), or Israelites (Exodus 31:13; 33:5 and countless more). The very same people were the recipients of the Torah on Mount Sinai. It is not correct to say that the Torah was given to the Jews because at that time the word 'Jew' was not even in existence and of course there were no Jews. One cannot find the word 'Jew' in the Hebrew Bible before the Babylonian captivity (Esther 2:5). In fact, the Torah was given to all the tribes of Israel, to the Hebrew nation.

In accordance with the will of God, it was said to King Solomon shortly before his death, "I will surely rend the kingdom from thee, and will give it to thy servant" (1 Kings 11:11). Immediately after Solomon's death in circa 930BCE, the United Kingdom of Israel was divided into the two separate, politically independent, often hostile states of Judea and Israel (the Ten Tribes). The northern Kingdom of Israel had lasted 209 years (930 BCE-721BCE). Israel was defeated and forced into Assyrian captivity circa 721BC and somehow mysteriously disappeared from the face of the earth. And so we read, "So Israel rebelled against house of David unto this day" (I Kings 12:19; II Chronicles 10:19), and "They and their fathers have transgressed against Me even unto this very day" (Ezekiel 2:3). The people of Israel became known as the legendary 'Ten Lost Tribes of Israel.'

Since the disappearance of the 'Lost' Ten Tribes, the world's chronological history has dealt with the remaining southern Kingdom of Judea, ignorant that the Jewish people represent the ancient Israel of the Biblical Twelve Tribes. Not so. Those Judeans have become identifiable as the Jewish People, the physical descendants of the Tribes of Judah, Benjamin and most of the tribe of Levy, collectively known to the world as the modern day Jews, whereas the tribe of Judah has always been dominant. Of course, it goes without saying that to be a Jew, one has to be born of a Jewish mother, have some Jewish ancestral background, or be properly converted to Judaism.

There are some scholars, even though they accept the concept of the existence of the Ten Tribes, for some strange, irrational reason call them 'Jews', as if they are indeed identifiable as the real physical descendants of Judah, Benjamin, and most of Levy. Of course, there is another understanding as to who might be called a 'Jew', beside what we just stated above, and that is abiding by the Jewish way of life and faith. The Ten Tribes have completely lost their Hebrew identity. They have forgotten the God of their fathers and His divine Torah. They have worshipped idols, the 'gods which cannot save'. To call them 'Jews' under these circumstances is sacrilege and insult against the Jews who worship the God of Israel and live by His holy Laws, who would rather sacrifice their life to keep their Jewish faith. It is very obvious that these criteria are not applicable to the Ten Tribes. To call them 'Jews' is historically incorrect and religiously unscriptural.

God chose the whole House of Israel long before they were divided into two groups of nations. Even once divided, the Almighty never expressed a preference for one Israelite nation over other. The Israelites have the same rights and obligations with respect to God and His Laws as the Jews. The Jews never abounded the Torah and have not lost their Jewish identity despite unspeakable suffering and persecution. Rather, they have become the most convicted witnesses of the existence of God: "You are My witnesses that I am God" (Isaiah 43:12). Meanwhile, the Ten Tribes, having being in exile for many long centuries by the God's design, have utterly lost their Israelite identity and knowledge of the divine Torah. But what is more important is that God has never rejected the Ten Tribes and broken His Covenant with them. Although Judah and Joseph have their own separate tasks to fulfill, they are equally included in God's Plan as His chosen people of Israel. God speaks to the people of Israel in terms that reaffirm His love and commitment: "I have chosen you, and not cast you away. Thou art My servant, O Israel, in whom I will be glorified" (Isaiah 41:9; 49:3).

The refusal of most rabbis and scholars to believe that the Ten Tribes—hundreds of millions Israelites—are still in exile is profoundly disturbing. Indeed, many academics and theologians ascribe to what is known as "Replacement Theory," according to which the Ten Tribes are a mere myth and fairytale. This theory has taken deep roots among not only the Jewish religious communities around the world, but in the secular circles in Israel and the

Diaspora as well. It purports that the Ten Tribes returned to the Promised Land in the time of the Prophets Jeremiah, Ezra, and Nehemiah; that Judah [the Jewish people] are the Biblical Israel representing all Twelve Tribes; and that all the future prophecies of reunification and redemption in the End Days pertain to them. These statements could not be further from the Biblical truth. The concept that the Ten Tribes of Israel were lost near three millennia ago and therefore have no part in the World-to-Come is entirely specious and has been rejected by God, the Sages of the Talmud, and secular and Rabbinical literature.

Despite all of the overwhelming evidence (especially the 'two sticks' of Ezekiel 37:15-28) to the contrary, the skeptics and deniers have rejected the plain truth of the Hebrew Bible and failed to differentiate between the meanings of the names Judah, Joseph, Israel, Jerusalem, Samaria, Ephraim, Manasseh, Jew—to them, they all mean 'Jew' and nothing else. They ignore the simple and clear teaching of the Restoration of the whole House of Jacob in the End Time; they do not pay proper attention to the way the Prophets of the Hebrew Bible have constantly made a careful distinction between the Kingdom of Israel and the Kingdom of Judah, and between the Israelite People and the Jewish People. The God of Israel has never said that Israel is Judah and Judah is Israel. He has dealt with these two Kingdoms and two nations completely separately throughout Scripture. The Jewish People and the Israelite People at this point in time are not synonymous, but different nations, living in very different parts of the world, having different histories, traditions, languages, cultures, and religions. And it will be that way until the advent of the Messiah and the realization of Redemption in the last days.

The great sage R. Nachmanides addresses the problems with so-called Replacement Theory and its variants. First of all, Nachmanides knew of the existence of the Ten Tribes and the countries of their residence. The Ten Tribes, he said in 1260CE, were still in Tserefath or Zarephath (France and its neighborhood) and 'at the ends of the north,' meaning at that time the northern areas of Europe. Many classical commentators of the Bible, such as Rashi, Daat Sofrim, Iben Ezra, and Radak, have supported his interpretation. R. Abarbanel believed that Zarephath also includes England, while the prophet Obadiah mentioned the children of Israel from Zarephath (1:20).

R. Nahmanides explains: "They [The Ten Tribes] are referred in a general sense as from Israel (2 Chronicles 35:18) and not by their specific tribes since they represented only a small portion of their tribe. These are they who returned under Esra with the Jews from Babylon. They were not expressly mentioned by their tribes since they were attached to Judah. They all settled in the cities of Judah. There was no Redemption for the Ten Tribes who remained in exile." That is why in the books of Ezra and Nehemiah only the families of Judah, Benjamin, and Levy [the Jewish people] are listed. R. Nachmanaides gives a strict and clarifying answer to those who deny the existence of the Ten Tribes in exile: *"There was no Redemption for the Ten Tribes who remained in exile"* (*Sefer HaGeulah*, The Book of Redemption, emphasis mine).

Much earlier, towards the end of the first century, the celebrated Jewish-Roman historian Flavius testified that the "The Ten Tribes are beyond the Euphrates until this day, and are an immense multitude whose numbers cannot be estimated" (Antiquities of the Jews, book XI, chapter 5:2). So, what happened to this 'immense multitude' of Israelites beyond the Euphrates and those of Zarephath (Europe)? Is it possible that they disappeared from the face of the earth without a trace?

Where Are the Ten Tribes Today?

Who are the Ten Tribes of Israel today and where are they geographically located? The Ten Tribes did not die out and disappear from history. It is the Word of God that all Twelve Tribes of the House of Israel will be represented among the nations in the End Times. Prophecy says that "Israel will multiply as the stars of the heaven and as the sand of the sea shore" (Genesis 22:17); the house of Israel will spread abroad to the four corners of the globe (Isaiah 11:12); God will be always with Israel, and bring them to the Holy Land again; all nations of the world will be blessed throughout Israel (Genesis 22:18); and God will not leave Israel until everything written and spoken will be done (Joshua 1:5; Deut. 31:6). Clearly, God is not speaking here only about the Jewish people, whose total population in the world today is only 13,746,000, of which 6,042,000 live in the State of Israel, while the rest (7,704,000) are scattered as a result of the Diaspora. And the Jews have had no nations and kingdoms of their own, except for Judaea in the past and the modern State of Israel today. Meanwhile, God predicted that "a nation and a company of nations shall be of thee [Israel], and kings shall come out of thy lions," vowing to "make of thee a multitude of people" (Genesis 35:11; 48:4). Surely, such words could not apply only to Judah, whose population (due to constant killings and holocausts) cannot approach the description of 'the stars of the sky and the sand of the seashore' which properly applies to the Ten Tribes of Israel. The total population of the house of Israel in the world, including the so-called 'Lost' Ten Tribes, is somewhere between 450,000,000 to 600,000,000 people!

Many historians and researchers have verified that the Israelite tribes are in our midst. Some of them reside in the most powerful countries of the world, such as United States of America (Manasseh), others live in formerly powerful countries such as

Britain (Ephraim), while others still live in Commonwealth and European countries such as Australia, Canada, New Zeeland, South Africa, Belgium, Denmark, Scotland, Ireland, Switzerland, Sweden, Finland, and Norway. They are all Israelite countries, originating from Israelite Tribes. Some of these countries have a large percentage of Israelites (or Hebrews) descent, others have smaller. Further information about the Ten Tribes is available through the Brit-Am, a movement of the Ten Tribes of Israel (visit their website at <http//hebrewnations.com>).

The United States and Great Britain have been close allies for many decades. The U.S in particular has aided the young Jewish state in times of need on many occasions. At the present time this brotherly special relationship between countries has severely deteriorated. Even this trend was prophesied in detail by the Bible: "They shall eat every man the flesh of his own arm: Manasseh, Ephraim; and Ephraim, Manasseh; and they together shall be against Judah" (Isaiah 9:21). Moreover, the prophecy of Zechariah illustrates precisely the geopolitical reality in the world today: "Then I cut asunder Mine other staff, even Bands, that I might break the brotherhood between Judah and Israel" (11:14). This division is precisely what is transpiring at the present moment in history: America and England are becoming increasingly hostile towards Judah, the State of Israel, and each other.

Various thinkers offer astute insight into the matter of Ten Tribes. The nineteenth-century Hebrew scholar R. Malbim anticipated that God would gather together the dispersed Ten Tribes in the future: "God will ingather the Ten Tribes who were in faraway lands and did not return in the time of the Second Temple." Several centuries before, the distinguished scholar R. Abarbanel also foresaw such a reunion: "The Ten Tribes will return to Samaria and its daughter-regions and so will the scattered dispersion of Judah be gathered in from the four corners of the earth. There is no doubt that this promised in gathering will occur in the Times of the Messiah. Until now it has never been fulfilled." To clarify, the question before these great Rabbis was whether the Ten Tribes would ever return to the Promised Land, not whether they had already returned. If the Ten Tribes have been lost to human history, not so with God. His words are self-evident and require no explanation: "Mine eyes are upon all their ways; they are not hid from My face" (Jeremiah 16:17). Throughout the Bible the prophets reinforced the intention of God to finally return the Ten Tribes to the status of chosen and blessed people again. Where the Ten Tribes are concerned, God's plan is plain: "I will say to them which were not My people, you are My people; and they shall say, You are my God" (Hosea 2:23); or "Judah and Israel will be as though I had not cast them off" (Zechariah 10:6).

As Rabbi Avraham Isaac Kook (1865-1935 CE) noted at the turn of the nineteenth century, those Israelites who were assimilated in ancient times, as well as their descendants, have gradually become more suited to receive the Divine Revelation of their Israelite identity. As time passes, they will yearn and strive to reclaim their Israelite inheritance (Shemoneh Kevatsim, Kovets 8:205).

One of the most crucial tasks that God has given to the Jewish people is to go to the countries and places where the Ten 'Lost' Tribes of Israel in exile reside (mainly in the West) and do everything possible to bring them back to the God of their fathers, to His everlasting Laws, and to the Promised Land. In fulfillment of this ambitious goal, the Jewish scholars and rabbis should enlighten the Israelites with the knowledge of God and kindle in their hearts the flame of love for the divine Torah, that its light may shine on them once more. The idea that the Jewish people are obliged by the Almighty to teach the lost Israelites the Torah and bring them back to the Holy Land finds its full support in the Tanakh, the Talmud, and the Rabbinical literature.

The Midrash (Yalkut Shimeoni on The Song of Solomon 1:16) fully supports and validates the prophesies regarding the future reunification of God's chosen people: "The Ten Tribes who were exiled beyond the Sambation River are they whom the exiled of Judah and Benjamin are destined to go unto and to bring them back in order to merit with them the days of the Messiah and life in the World-to-Come, as it says. *'In those days the House of Judah shall go unto the House of Israel, and they shall come together out of the land of the north to the land I have given for an inheritance unto their fathers'* (Jeremiah 3:18, emphasis mine). Another Midrash that speaks of the importance of Israelite unity says: "And you find that Israel will not be redeemed until they become one unity" (Tanchuma, Nitzavim 1:18, reflecting on Jeremiah 3:18 and Ezekiel 37:22).

To all the deniers of the existence of the Ten Tribes still in exile and their future return, including 'the citizens of Jerusalem' of old (see Ezekiel 12:15), R. Akiva, and various rabbis, scholars, and other skeptics, the God of Israel responds: "Although I have cast them far off among the heathen, and although I have scattered them among the countries, yet will I be to them as a little sanctuary in the countries where they shall come. I will even gather you from the people, and assemble you out of the countries where you have been scattered, and I will give you the land of Israel. *And they shall be My people, and I will be their God"* (Ezekiel 11:15-20, emphasis mine)! To this powerful message we may add, that it is forbidden to be amongst those who deny the Redemption of the Ten Tribes.

The Hebrew Scripture also offers ample confirmation of the future reality of reunification. The greatest prophecy of the Bible is the prediction of the final ingathering and redemption of the nations of Judah and Israel in the latter years of the advent of the Messiah. This 'Great Exodus' of all Twelve Tribes of Israel will be much greater than the miraculous return of the Jews in 1948, and even greater than the exodus from Egypt under Moses in circa 1300BCE. In order for these prophecies to be fulfilled, the Ten Tribes of Israel will need to have repented, reunited with Judah, and turned to the God of Israel and His Immortal Torah. All of this things will be accomplished in due time in the 'days of Mashiah.' We have no doubt that "The counsel of the Lord stands forever, the plan of His heart to all generations" (Psalms 33:11).

The divine presence of God, *Shekhinah*, follows the Ten Tribes in Exile and 'hovers over Israel like a mother over her children.' Thus we read: "Wheresoever they were exiled, the *Shekhinah* went with them" (Megillah 29a). As Joseph revealed his identity with a loud cry to his shocked brothers in the land of Egypt (Genesis 45:1-2), so it will be in the future when the descendants of Joseph, who represent the Ten Tribes, come to Judah for reunification: "With cries they will come, and with mercy I will lead them" (Jeremiah 31:8). As in the past, the Jewish nation will be taken aback to see this magnificent Exodus of a multitude of Israelites coming to join them. Their hearts will be thrilled and exult with joy, and their eyes will shine. In the Biblical description of this touching moment, "Then shalt thou say in thine heart, who hath begotten me these, seeing I have lost my children, and am desolate, a captive, and removing to and fro? And who hath brought up these? Behold, I was left alone; these, where had they been" (Isaiah 49:21).

As Arthur Schopenhauer, a German philosopher (1788-1860 CE) rightfully noted, "All truth passes through three stages: First it is ridiculed. Second, it is violently opposed. Third, it is accepted as being self-evident." Indeed, the self-evident truth is that, despite ridicule and opposition of the idea, the Twelve Tribes of Israel will be restored and redeemed as one nation united by one King, the Messiah son of David. Through this unified and redeemed nation of Israel all the divine blessings of the Bible will come to pass in this world, as it is written: "All people on earth will be blessed through you" (Genesis 12:31). This ancient prophecy will find its complete fulfillment only in the Messianic Time, when justice and peace will finally prevail and knowledge of God will cover the earth. The time is coming when Israel, the servant of God, will be rewarded for their righteousness.

As one nation of Priests, the Light to the world, the Israelites and their Messiah will teach and guide the nations to worship the one and the only God of the Universe, the God of Israel, by demonstrating God's righteousness, holiness, and love to all the inhabitants of the earth, in order that all might merit life together in the wonderful World-to-Come that is the purpose of all Creation.